Look at the Sky

GEORGE D. DURRANT
WITH A CHAPTER BY DWIGHT Q. DURRANT

BOOKCRAFT
Salt Lake City, Utah

Library of Congress Catalog Card Number: 94-70746
ISBN 0-88494-925-7

First Printing, 1994

Printed in the United States of America

To all, and particularly to
those who
teach:

The words of
the Apostle Paul
offer the
key to
seeing life's
beautiful sky.

He reminds us that no matter
what is included in our possessions,
our accomplishments,
or our lives,
if we do not have
a certain something, then
nothing else matters,
for he said that
if we "have not charity,
[we are] nothing. . . .
Charity suffereth long, and is kind;
charity envieth not;
charity vaunteth not itself, is not puffed up,
doth not behave itself unseemly,
seeketh not her own,
is not easily provoked,
thinketh no evil;
rejoiceth not in iniquity,
but rejoiceth in the truth. . . .
Charity never faileth."

Contents

Contents

1

Why Don't You Look at the Sky?

I've been told that a traveler driving through Manti, Utah, stopped, rolled down his car window, and asked a farmer unlocking a gate near the road, "How do I get to Salt Lake City from here?"

The farmer replied: "You can go up several miles, then turn left and go through Moroni, and continue on to Nephi. Get on the freeway and head north to Salt Lake City. Or you can go past the turnoff and go up through Thistle and then down Spanish Fork Canyon to the freeway. Go north and you'll get to Salt Lake City."

After considering the alternatives, the visitor asked, "Does it matter which way I go?"

The farmer, who now had the gate opened, replied, "Not to me it don't."

Some things don't really matter, but other things matter a lot.

For example, directions for getting to some places could be confusing for a time, but eventually you'd get there; in the end, it doesn't really matter what route you take or which directions you follow. However, the directions you follow to arrive at happiness matter a lot, because if you go the wrong way you may never get there. The directions to happiness matter more than the directions to any other destination. Sometimes as we travel through life we get confused, take some unwise turns, and begin to travel the wrong way—the way to unhappiness.

The consequences of going the wrong way are illustrated in this story:

Two beginning but lucky deer hunters had shot a big buck. They were dragging it to camp when an experienced hunter coming up the trail observed that they were pulling it by its hind legs. He helpfully suggested, "If you fellers will pull that deer by its horns, you will be dragging it with the grain of the hair and it will go more easily."

Taking this advice, the hunters took hold of the horns and dragged the deer for another hour. Finally one said to the other, "He was right; it does drag easier this way."

"Yes," replied the other, "but we are getting farther and farther away from camp."

Often we, like those two deer hunters, become confused in our direction. We move ahead, only to learn that the things we are doing are leading us away from rather than toward where we want to be. Thus we move farther and farther away from the fulfillment, the security, and the joy of our longed-for camp. We become lost in the foreground of life—the frustrations, the details, the competitions, the duties, the seeming necessities, the so-called "fun." And finding ourselves in the midst of these things, we lose all sense of direction. It is then that we need to look up and see the sky. In doing so we can find the bearings that will help us adjust our direction and get us on the right road—the road to happiness.

I'm an artist, you know. You may not have known that. Well, you need to come over to my house and see my watercolor paintings. I'm sure that because you are nice and generous, when you look at my works you will say, "Wow! Those are beautiful." Of course they really aren't that good, but I'm getting better.

I recall the first art class I took, way back in my early college days. It took all the confidence I could muster just to enroll. I knew that everyone else in the class would be Leonardo da Vincis and I'd suffer much self-inflicted humiliation as I compared my meager abilities with theirs.

I did my first painting for the class in watercolors. It turned out a little better than I thought it might when I first put the paint on the paper. Even so, I was shocked and filled with fear when the teacher announced, "I see that most of you have completed your first painting. So let's all put them up here along the wall. When they are all in place we will criticize one another's work."

I thought to myself, *I didn't know I'd have to put my picture up to be criticized. If I had known that, I would have never taken this class.*

But having no choice, I reluctantly put my picture on the far right of the display. I hoped that the criticism would begin with the pictures on the left side and maybe the class time would end before it was my turn. Or I hoped at least they'd use up all their criticisms on the other paintings before they got to mine.

As the discussions of the first few paintings were taking place, I didn't say anything about anybody else's efforts. I hoped my silence would indicate that I had no desire to criticize their work, and then, if they were Christians, they wouldn't say anything about mine.

But the clock moved so slowly and the discussion so rapidly that with five minutes remaining, all eyes except mine focused on my work. My insecurities made it so that I could not muster the courage to look up. As everyone looked at my painting, there were several seconds of silence.

Then I heard a girl's voice. In a quiet, kindly tone she said, "I like the sky." Those four words gave me a small feeling of confidence. I lifted my eyes and looked up at the painting. To myself I said, *By George, that* is *a nice sky.*

From the other side of the room, a fellow spoke up. "But he has got the foreground all fouled up."

In my mind I responded, *Why don't you look at the sky?*

And then I thought, *Next time he won't be able to say such a thing, because next time my foreground will be as good as my sky.*

So now, many years after that experience, I say to all of you and to myself what I said then: Why don't *we* look at the sky—and then go to work and beautify our foreground so it will be like our sky.

To you whose foreground is colored with muddy gray meanness, I say: Look up at the sky and see what you ought to be, what you could be. Then begin to paint into your foreground some bright-colored kindness. As you do so, you'll be headed toward happiness.

To you whose habits and behavior are degrading, I say: Look up and see the purity of the true blue of your sky. Paint your foreground with colors that will show your loyalty to your family, to God, and to yourself. Then you'll see a road sign saying Happiness This Way.

To you whose foreground is painted with the drab colors of discouragement and despair, I say: Look up to the light of the sky and see the hope there. Paint yourself some new goals, goals that will lead you through the density of a self-pitying foreground and onto the path of hope.

To you who have painted your foreground with thick jungles of sins that cling to you like the snags of life's thistles, I say: Look up. An upward gaze will give you the desire to wipe life's paper clean and to begin to paint a path that will get you through to a happier place.

Yes, there are some things that matter a lot—a whole lot.

Looking up at the sky is perhaps among the ultimate of those things. Looking up is closely related to having charity, and as the Apostle Paul said, "Charity never faileth." Looking up at the sky can symbolize seeing and loving the good, and seeing and loving God. When we see the good in ourselves and in others, we will see the direction that will move us ever closer to that which matters most—happiness.

This book is about life. But to limit its pages I shall speak mainly about teaching. To discuss teaching is to discuss the very central and binding essence of life. What I say of teaching can be expanded to include every relationship we have with others, and it is in our relationships with others that we find misery or joy.

Teachers are those who teach facts and things, and that matters. But what matters most is for a teacher to stand in the foreground with those who are looking around and to point out to them the direction to happiness. Teachers are those who say, "I know your life's journey can be hard, but, my friend, let me show you something. Come here and stand by me. Look up; see the sky. Can you see up there what you can learn? Can you see what you could feel? Can you see the beauty of what you are? Can you see the glory of what you can be? You can go up there, you know. I'm your teacher; I'm your friend. I can help you get up there. Now, let's get going down that right path. It won't be easy, but we've got directions. We know where happiness is, and together we are going to make it."

Yes, that is a teacher. Not just a teacher, but a master teacher—a teacher who makes a difference.

As I told you earlier, I'm an artist, though not at all a renowned one. For me, being a good artist doesn't really matter.

But I'm also a teacher. And oh, how I long to be a good teacher, because being a good teacher, a teacher who helps students see the sky, matters a lot. Being that kind of teacher means being a master teacher. And to be a master teacher is my fondest desire.

Those who know me might say, "But you aren't really a master teacher." To that I'd reply: Well, I try. I really do. But of course it's difficult. Still, I dream of it. I even dream that someday my tombstone will read, "GEORGE DONALD DURRANT—A GOOD HUSBAND, A GOOD FATHER"—and in very small print—"a master teacher." If that inscription were so recorded, I'd probably sneak back from the spirit world and change my epitaph to read, "He wanted to be a master teacher."

A valid criterion to determine if you or I, who are teachers, deserve such an accolade as "master teacher" would be the statement:

"This teacher helped the students look up and see the sky and helped them find the road to happiness."

2

The Day the Sky Almost Fell

Oh, how I wanted to be a seminary teacher! I felt nothing else would do for me. If prayer could make it so, then I'd definitely be a seminary teacher.

I arose from my knees, looked in the bedroom mirror, straightened my tie, put on my suit coat, and walked out of my wife's and my small apartment into the summer sun.

At that time, the administrative offices of the seminary program were located in the Karl G. Maeser Building on the Brigham Young University campus. The journey from our front door was less than half a mile. Even walking at a slow pace I would arrive five minutes early for my 3:30 appointment.

As I walked along I scarcely realized where I was, for my mind was filled to overflowing with the significance of the impending interview. It would decide whether my fondest dream would come true. My stomach had the light, fluttering feeling one feels only when standing on the edge of an opportunity to win or lose a most cherished prize. This 3:30 appointment with this certain man would not last more than ten minutes, but in that fateful bit of time my future would be decided. Either I'd be a seminary teacher or I'd . . . I could not bear to consider what else I might be.

The pounding of my heart was not caused by climbing up the stairs that led up the hill to the seminary program offices. I knew I must calm down or else my nerves would render my mind a useless mass.

As my hand reached out to clutch the handle on the west door of the Maeser Building, I paused before pulling the door toward me. I silently prayed for success. I took three deep breaths and then pulled the door open.

When I entered the suite of offices, the receptionist greeted me warmly by saying, "Oh, you must be George Durrant. Is that right?"

For a moment it was as if I weren't quite sure whether I was him or not. Finally I muttered, "Yes, I am."

She said, "He has someone else with him right now, George, but that should only be for a few more minutes. Just have a seat over there."

I sat down. As I reached for a magazine I noticed that my hand was trembling. I opened the cover and looked inside, but I didn't read. I couldn't. I could scarcely breathe.

Finally the man came out with another fellow, and they bade each other good-bye.

"George Durrant is here for his appointment," the receptionist said cheerfully.

"Come in, Brother Durrant," he said in a pleasant yet serious tone.

I stood up and followed him into his office.

"Have a chair," he said, pointing to one. I sat down and felt grateful the chair had two wooden arms that my trembling hands could clutch.

Without any talk of the weather or world events or sports, he looked into my eyes and asked sincerely, "So you want to be a seminary teacher?"

"Ye—" I cleared my throat and started over. "Yes, I do."

"Why?"

Never had I been so well prepared to answer a question. But my mind was so clouded by fears that I couldn't express my thoughts.

"Well," I began. I cleared my throat again. "Well, I, uh . . . I just think that would be good. I could study the gospel, and I just think that I'd be a . . . well, a good teacher and live a happy life if I was a seminary teacher." I don't know what else I said. But I could tell he was not impressed (and neither was I), and that caused me to lose even the small portion of confidence I had had. My countenance dimmed and I fell silent.

He was kind, but I could tell it was over. I had failed. As he led the way to the door he shook my hand and said, "We have many more applicants than we do jobs. But if you want, the secretary will give you an application form and you can fill it out in case something comes up in the future. You never know." I knew he was saying this just to try to restore me to some degree of self-respect.

As the receptionist handed me the form, I looked away. I felt so very bad. So very worthless. Going down the hill seemed symbolic of the direction of my life. I couldn't understand why I could be a reasonably radiant personality almost all the time, yet whenever I was interviewed for something that really mattered I couldn't be myself.

In a few minutes I was home. My wife, Marilyn, had just returned from her job at the telephone company. She sensed my disappointment and asked, "It didn't go well at the interview?"

Looking away from her, I painfully replied, "No . . . no, it didn't. It won't . . ." I could say no more.

Trying to buoy me up, she said, "Well, you can teach art like you'd planned before you went in the army." But then, as she opened the fridge to get out a package of hamburger, she looked at me and softly said, "It's too bad for the seminary kids, because you would have been the best seminary teacher in the whole world."

She smiled, turned toward the cupboard to get a mixing bowl, and said, "Isn't that right?"

I almost smiled as I replied, "That's right."

After dinner Marilyn hurried off to an evening genealogy class and I was left alone to ponder. My seminary sky had fallen. My great question was, what now?

3

Remembering the Times When I'd Been Shown the Sky

After dinner, try as I would I could not remove from my mind and heart the despair of losing my dream. Marilyn had hurried off to her class, and I lingered at the table, feeling too discouraged to attack any meaningful activity. I silently prayed for strength. The answer I received was in the form of an idea, and the idea was to do the dishes. So I stood up and began the exhilarating task of dishwashing. When I had finished I felt the joy of having made a difference, for the kitchen looked much better now.

That good feeling gave me another idea—to go for a walk. I left the uncomfortably warm apartment and was soon on the sidewalk. As I moved along I considered over and over again the question, "Why do you want to be a seminary teacher?" Now my mind was overflowing with the answer, and oh, how

I longed for a second chance to respond! To myself I said, *I'll tell you why I want to be a seminary teacher—because I love young people and I want to help them learn some things that I have learned.*

It was as simple as that. I didn't want to be a seminary teacher because that would be a good life for me. I wanted to be a seminary teacher so that I could help young people have good lives. To myself I then said, *I wish I had told him that I want to help young people as my teachers have helped me.* But then a most wonderful thought came into my mind: *I don't have to be a seminary teacher to do what I want to do. I just have to be a teacher.*

My eyes welled up with tears at this heartfelt insight. I suddenly knew all would be well, for I knew that my lot in life was to be a teacher—any kind of teacher who would associate with young people. Maybe an elementary school teacher. Maybe an art teacher. Maybe a history teacher. Maybe a coach. It didn't matter what I taught; all that mattered was that I would teach. That insight into my destiny chased away all discouragement and filled my heart with precious hope.

As I walked along, my mind was flooded with remembrances of my past teachers. *Perhaps . . .* , I said to myself, *perhaps I can be to some young people what some of my teachers have been to me.*

I smiled as I thought back some fifteen years to Mr. Brimhall. He was my fifth-grade teacher at the old Harrington Elementary School in American Fork.

Mr. Brimhall acted as if he was so mean. That memory caused a broad smile to cross my face. I too thought he was mean back then. I recalled that some said, "Mr. Brimhall is mean. But he's fair, because he's mean to *everybody.*"

But, you know, I said to myself, *he wasn't mean at*

all. How could a mean teacher have been so kindly aware of an insecure little guy like me? How could a mean teacher have said to me almost every day, "George, it's a little noisy out in the hall. You are our official door-closer. Would you get up and go close the door?"

At this request I would go to the door, close it, and return to my seat. Mr. Brimhall would say, "Thank you, George. You are a good door-closer." I'd feel as though I were the most important person in the class and maybe even in the whole world, and that Mr. Brimhall was the world's kindest man.

I knew that being asked to close the door didn't have anything to do with arithmetic. I seldom could have been praised for my prowess in that area. But I knew Mr. Brimhall was right—I was a good door-closer. And somehow that made up for a lot of things I wasn't so good at.

One day we were studying fractions. Mr. Brimhall said, "If you had four quarters of a pie, they would all be equal in size." He added, "The four quarters of anything are all equal in size."

I raised my hand and, mustering all my courage, said, "Mr. Brimhall, that's not right."

"Oh?" he said in sort of a mean way. "When is it not right?"

I timidly replied, "Well, my dad shot a deer, and I was helping him cut it up. The hindquarters were a lot bigger than the front ones."

The twenty-nine other students all laughed at my remark. I suddenly found myself wishing I'd kept quiet as I usually did.

Mr. Brimhall didn't laugh. He stood up from his chair and walked over to where I sat. He stood above me, put his hand on my shoulder, and softly said, "I've never thought of it like that. You are absolutely right. George, you've got what I call common sense, and that is the best kind of sense."

I had lowered my head when all the other students had laughed at what I'd said. But when Mr. Brimhall said that, I looked up, and in a sense I saw the sky.

I'll always remember that moment when a kind teacher who knew something about the insecurity of a little boy caused me to look up. In a small way, from that moment on I was never quite the same.

The memories of Mr. Brimhall caused me to focus on my vision even more clearly. I knew more certainly that I wanted to be, in my own way, a Mr. Brimhall. I wanted to be a teacher.

As I rambled along in my evening walk, I grew more excited at the prospect of teaching.

Suddenly, and gently, Mr. Sorensen appeared in my mind. He was smiling as he always did ten years earlier when I was a ninth grader. Mr. Sorensen had grown up in Sanpete County, Utah, and he had a country-type wit and the kind of wisdom that is peculiar to those who grow up around horses, cows, barns, and irrigation ditches.

I recalled my first day in his class. He called me by name, and because of the way he looked at me, I sensed that perhaps I had a shot at being his favorite. I'd not had much luck through the years at becoming a teacher's favorite, even though I'd longed to be that as much as I'd ever longed to be anything.

The second day of class Mr. Sorensen told a story that made me laugh so hard I thought I'd fall out of my chair. He said in his slow sort of drawl: "Down in Sanpete County there were these two guys who went hunting for birds. One of the two stuttered and the other shook. Well, they saw a bird and argued over who would shoot it. The one who shook was carrying the gun, and so they finally decided that he'd shoot. As he aimed, the gun's barrel shook back and forth. Shaking even more, he aimed . . . and then he aimed a bit longer. Finally he fired and the bird fell. He shouted, 'I got it! I got it!' His friend said, 'Well, you-you-you should have. You-you-you aimed at the whole tree!' "

That night at dinnertime I told my family the story. They laughed some, but not nearly as much as I did.

As the days went by I'd tell Mom nearly every night what Mr. Sorensen had said that day. I remember her saying, "George, you sure do seem to like that Mr. Sorensen." I could tell that Mom liked him too, because parents really like teachers whom their children like.

Remembering those pleasant experiences filled my heart with joy. But then I remembered a most troubling experience I had with Mr. Sorensen.

Two weeks into that same school year a major crisis came into my life. The principal sent a note saying that there were two too many students in Mr. Sorensen's history class and that another teacher didn't have enough students. Thus, two students were going to have to transfer from the large class to the small one.

Mr. Sorensen looked sad as he told us the news. I could tell he didn't want to lose any of us. He said, "To make this fair I'll choose two numbers between one and thirty-five. Then you can each write a number on a piece of paper and give it to me. The two of you who choose the number closest to the two numbers I have chosen will be the ones who will move."

I had a feeling I'd be one of those who would choose an unlucky number. Just the thought of that caused me deep pain.

I watched Mr. Sorensen write down the two numbers, and it seemed to me that he wrote two digits for each number. Therefore, I felt that each of the two numbers had to be ten or higher. If I wrote the number one on my paper, I'd be far away from the dreaded numbers and I wouldn't have to move.

Finally, having gathered and studied the numbers, Mr. Sorensen announced that the numbers he had written were twenty-five and one. He continued, "Betty, you chose twenty-four, so you are to go." Then he paused as his eyes focused on me. "And George, you chose the number one, so you'll go too."

I hadn't cried in many years, and I didn't want to cry then. But I couldn't hold back such a flood of emotions. I didn't cry out loud, but every person in the class could tell what I was doing.

Mr. Sorensen was almost always jovial, but at that moment I could tell he wasn't too far from tears himself.

My classmates became sober on seeing my distress. Silence filled the classroom. After several seconds I heard a girl's voice say, "Mr. Sorensen, Betty and I are friends. I'll go with her and George can stay here."

Mr. Sorensen smiled and said, "Did you hear that, George? Are you willing to stay here with an old codger like me and let Anna go to that other wonderful class?"

I had been looking down so my classmates wouldn't see my tears. But what Mr. Sorensen said caused me to look up. I said in a whisper, "Yeah, I'll stay here." I sniffed, and added, a little more loudly, "I'm willing to stay with you, Mr. Sorensen." He smiled and nodded his approval.

That sort of sealed it, I guess. Mr. Sorensen and I had been close before, but now we were fast friends.

I'd never had a teacher before who was my friend. Oh, he wasn't a friend like my friends Bob and Don L. and Delmar, because he was a teacher. But he treated me like a true friend. I'd come to class as early as I could so that he and I could talk about sports and World War II. He'd tell me stuff just as though I were another teacher. He seemed to respect me, even though I'm sure he knew that that year was a troubled time for me—a time when I didn't have much respect for myself. A time when I did a lot of looking down because of my insecurities. A time when I needed someone to tell me often to look up at the sky.

As I walked along I shook my head and said out loud, "I don't know what would have happened to me if Mr. Sorensen hadn't been there pointing the way. He mattered. He mattered a lot."

I'd walked farther than I'd intended, but with every step I was gaining more and more enthusiasm for the future. Art! That was what I'd teach. Art!

Thinking of art unleashed a new set of memories. I'd wanted to take art classes in high school, but my friends (who controlled much of what I did in those days) didn't look upon that with much favor, so because of pressure from them I steered clear of the turpentine-smelling art room.

My art career didn't really get started until I was in college. Strangely enough, it started in a sociology class. That was the first college class—or any class, for that matter—in which I sat on the front row.

My sociology teacher had said something controversial—I believe he did so just to get a reaction out of the students. But when he asked if anyone wanted to comment on what he had said, the class was silent.

I wanted to say something because I didn't agree with him, but I never made comments in my classes except when I wanted to be goofy and make people laugh.

Now, this class was filled with more than eighty students, and for that reason I had never said a word during the semester. So naturally I didn't comment. The teacher asked again, "Any comments?" I felt a great urge to speak up, but my lack of courage would not allow me to do so.

The teacher paused.

And suddenly, almost against my will, I was speaking. My words were coming from my heart, and my whole body seemed to vibrate with nervous energy.

Everyone listened while I tried to make my point. When I finished, the teacher asked, "What is your name?"

I replied, "George."

"George who?"

"George Durrant."

"Students, did you all hear what George Durrant said?"

Soon the class discussion moved on, but I kept thinking over and over about the teacher's words: "Students, did you all hear what George Durrant said?"

That was the highlight of my college career.

Two days later I went to this same teacher's office to see him. I wondered if I should quit school, because I had no real direction in my life. I didn't know whom to go to for help. But this teacher's name kept coming to me, and so I mustered all my courage and approached his door.

I knocked and heard him shout gruffly, "Come in!" I opened the door and looked in. When he saw me he smiled, stood up, shook my hand, and said, "Sit down, my friend."

We talked. After several moments, he put his feet up on another chair and we talked some more.

He didn't seem to want to talk about sociology— he just seemed to want to talk about me.

"What are you majoring in?" he asked.

"I'm not sure," I replied.

"Well, what are you good at?"

"Nothing, I guess."

"Come on, George," he said warmly. "A guy like you has to be good at a lot of things."

"Well," I said shyly and with a touch of humor, "when I was a little kid I could keep the Crayolas in the lines."

He laughed, then pulled his chair close to mine, looked into my eyes, and said, "Then why don't you major in art? You could do it. A guy like you can do anything you want to do. You've got what it takes." He treated me as if I were of royal blood—me, an insecure young guy, and he acted as if I were a real somebody. That day in his office he took the time to say in his own way: "Look up, George. Way up there. That's you up there."

So that was it. Because of that teacher I would set out to be an artist. And I've discovered you don't have to be what you set out to be—the important thing is that you set out.

As I continued my walk, I considered in amazement the influence that teacher had on my life.

Could I ever have such an influence on anyone? I wondered. I looked up into the sky, gazed at the stars just coming out, and hoped.

4

Saved by the Helicopter in the Sky

I sensed I had walked far enough. I turned and headed back toward home, my mind continuing its excited consideration of the future. But then, as on so many occasions, my enthusiasm became dampened as reality took center stage.

I recalled my rather harrowing student-teaching experience that had taken place some three years earlier. Before I was drafted into the army I had intended to be an art teacher. I had done my student teaching at my old high school in American Fork.

I've never been as keyed up and nervous as I was on that winter day when three other college students and I drove from BYU to American Fork. Once at the school the four of us went our separate ways. I walked down the hall, up the stairs, and to the art room where Mr. Nelson, the art teacher, greeted me.

He beckoned me to come in. When he introduced me to the students, I could see no glee in any of their eyes. They seemed to care very little that I was there. As a matter of fact, they seemed to care very little about anything that I cared a lot about.

For the next two days I sat in the back of the classroom and watched, feeling as much out of place as I had ever felt. The class conduct was not exemplary, and my hopes for success faded fast.

The vast majority of the students in the class had been kicked out of other classes and had all been collected together in the art room. The school counselor seemed to have the notion that there was no way to fail in art.

Finally my time to teach was just a weekend away. Mr. Nelson told me he felt I would do best if he wasn't in the classroom at all. The class was the first hour of the morning, and so he said he'd just come to school an hour late each day. I was both sad and glad he wouldn't be there—sad because I feared what this group of rebels might do without his firm hand to quell any riots, but glad because I felt that indeed I'd do better without any interference.

The unit I would teach would be on the subject I had the most confidence in—watercolor.

That weekend was torturous for me as I considered where I'd be on Monday morning. To add to my distress, on Saturday morning my supervising teacher from BYU called me and told me that Monday was the only day that he could come to evaluate my effectiveness, and so he'd be there.

Sunday night was mostly a sleepless one. Morning came, and the four of us made the drive to American Fork. Needless to say, I rode along in silence.

I had hoped we'd arrive thirty minutes before

class was to begin. But due to six inches of newly fallen snow our journey took longer than usual, and school would start in five minutes. As I walked from the parking lot to the school building I was a bit more shaken.

I hurried up the stairs to the art room. I was glad that on Friday I had arranged all the supplies in just the right order for me to do my demonstration and for the students to begin their work. As nervous as I was, I was certain that all would go reasonably well because I was so well prepared.

As I entered the art room I saw three senior boys and a junior girl standing by an open window. I opened the desk drawer to get the key for the cabinets where I had all the supplies ready. But the key was not there. I literally ransacked the drawer, throwing things every direction as I searched for the key.

Seeing my frantic action, the tallest of the three boys asked, "What are you looking for, Mr. Durrant?"

"The key to the cabinet!" I shouted back.

"Oh hey, you mean the one Carl threw out the window into the snow."

"Don't blame it on me," said Carl. "You guys are the ones who dropped it."

I went to the window and looked down. My first thought was to rush out and dig in the snow. But there was no time, and besides, such a venture offered little hope for success.

The bell rang, and I'm sure my face, which had been red with anger, was now white with fear—as white as the snow that covered the key. That key would have opened the door to success, but now it would open me up for my greatest failure.

"Good morning, Mr. Durrant," my supervising teacher said as he came up to my side unnoticed.

"Oh yeah, good morning."

"I'll just sit in the back and watch a master teacher at work. Don't worry about me; you'll do fine."

In my nervous condition I could scarcely even call the roll, but as I did I wondered, *What can I do?*

As I called Sam Walker's name I saw a piece of charcoal on the desk. I looked over at the easel and saw a large block of newsprint paper there.

After calling the last name on the roll I nervously announced, "Students, this week we will work on drawing."

"Oh good," a boy at the back said mockingly. "Maybe that will help me win the new car this summer in the 'Steel Day' drawing."

A fellow in the front shouted, "He doesn't mean that kind of drawing, stupid."

By now I had placed the easel and the paper in the front of the room.

"Let's see," I said. "Let's draw a house and a fence and some trees. First the house."

As I drew I said, "We need to get the perspective just right. There, that looks pretty good. Now, in a charcoal drawing you only have black and white and all the values in between. So first let's do some parts of the house in black."

I then asked, "If it was daytime, what parts of the house would be the darkest?"

I hoped they'd say the windows, but to my dismay the guy in the back, the one who I believe had thrown out the key, said, "Straight down the old chimney."

Everyone laughed, because he really was a funny guy.

I couldn't restrain myself from chuckling a little. "Good comment, Herman! That would be exactly right if we were hovering over the house in a helicopter."

I smiled, and everyone could see the logic in both Herman's comment and my response.

By now I was feeling quite comfortable. The drawing went well. There were many catcalls coming from those who wanted to be noticed, but I didn't mind. It's hard to disrupt an art class, especially when a genius like me is at the old easel.

I finished the drawing just before the bell rang. I had survived. I hadn't been a great success, but I had avoided failure.

When the students were gone the supervising teacher came up and said, "Good job, George. When you responded with the helicopter answer I wrote in my notes, 'Give him an A.' "

I walked out of the school that day without my feet ever touching the ground. I seemed to soar as I moved from the school building to the car. I was having one of those moments that only teachers can know, filled with unsurpassed joy.

I wanted more of those moments. I wanted to be a teacher.

But for the teacher, today's successes or failures are soon pushed aside by the preparation for tomorrow. Now it was tomorrow, and I was teaching again.

Three boys were grouped together in the back, and they had all left their papers white and untouched. I walked over to them and said, "Hey, guys, how about all of us getting busy? What do you say?" The two boys who were standing returned to their seats and were soon drawing, but the third, with whom the other two had been visiting, just sat staring out the window. There was an empty seat by him and so I sat down.

"Jay," I said, "I hear that you can really throw the javelin."

He didn't respond.

"Is that right?" I asked.

"That's right," he said in a tone that indicated he didn't want to talk.

"Do you think the snow will be melted so they can hold the meet this Friday?" He didn't reply. I continued, "It looks like it. It's warm out today. If they hold the meet I'm coming to see you throw."

He still hadn't looked at me, and I sensed I should move on. I was disappointed he hadn't responded.

As I moved away I could see him begin to draw something on his paper.

The next day something happened that I shall never forget.

I called the roll, and when I was nearly finished a girl came in late. I gently said, "Welcome, Betty." She slammed her book down on her desk.

I spoke again: "Betty, don't get too comfortable yet. You need to go to the office and get an admit slip."

"What for?" she said with disgust.

"Because you missed class yesterday, and you know you must get an admit slip." With that she stood up and walked to the front. She stood close to me and almost shouted as she said, "I'll tell you what you can do with your admit slips." She proceeded to shout obscenities at me that I hadn't heard since my army days.

Betty was in a rage to the point that it twisted her otherwise beautiful face. I, of course, as her vocabulary at the time dwarfed mine, was speechless. I knew immediately that she was not having her best day so far and that she was bound and determined to keep me from having my best day too.

Having finished her tirade, she stormed out of the door and slammed it closed.

"Don't mind her," Herman said. "She explodes like an atom bomb every once in a while. It's not your fault."

The class seemed to be sobered by what had happened. Somehow I sensed her attack had caused them to feel closer to me. I felt a surge of love for them. It seems that as students and their teacher go through things together it can make them feel a common bond with each other.

After class I went down to the office and asked the secretary if the girl had come there.

"Oh yes, she did," the secretary answered. "She's got a lot of problems at home that she can't cope with, so once in a while she acts a bit berserk. I understand she shouted at you. If you want we'll put her in the class she was in before—that's where she should be, but it wasn't working out so well, and we thought we'd try art."

"No, I don't want her to leave. Maybe I can help. At least, I'd like to try."

"All right. Good luck."

Friday I went to the track meet. The spring snow had melted, and it was a beautiful day. I saw Jay throw the javelin.

The next Monday, after class had begun, I went back to where he sat. He surprised me by speaking to me first.

"Did you come to see me throw?" he asked.

I nodded my head up and down and sort of smiled a prideful smile as I said, "I was there, all right. I saw you run forward and then rear back and let it go. I watched that javelin sail up into the clear blue sky, and as I watched it fly farther and farther I said to myself, I don't think that thing will ever come down."

He looked into my eyes, and something went

between us. Something that can go between people. Something good that happens sometimes between students and teachers.

After a few seconds of silence Jay spoke again.

"Look at this drawing of this house and fence and trees. It don't look quite right. What can I do to make it better?"

"Well, my friend," I replied, "the sky looks good. But right here in the foreground . . ."

Oh, the girl! She was there every day. She didn't tell me she was sorry, but she didn't swear at me anymore. Even if she had I'd still have wanted her in there. After all, there weren't any signs on the wall saying Don't Swear at the Teacher.

When my time was up and I told my students good-bye, she smiled at me. And to me, that was apology enough.

My student teaching was over. I received an A for my grade because of the helicopter answer. But I really deserved a C because I was pretty average— except for just once in a while when for a minute or two I'd be pretty darn good, and my students and I would catch a glimpse of the sky.

I'd learned a lot while teaching that interesting assortment of students. The main thing I'd learned was that maybe, just maybe, I could be a pretty good teacher. I sure did want to do that. But first there was the army and Korea, and that changed a lot of things for me.

I quickened my pace to get back home. I'd done enough thinking for now.

5

The Subject Matter May Change, But Not the Sky

Soon my walk was over, and I was home. When Marilyn came back from her class we began to talk. She was a bit surprised by my obvious happiness, and she listened closely as I described, as best as I could, the thoughts that had come to me as I had walked. Finally I had expressed all the feelings that I had, and I said, "So I've decided it doesn't matter as much what I teach as it matters that I simply teach."

"But," she replied, as though she wasn't quite convinced, "your heart was so set on being a seminary teacher. You told me of your experiences while you served in the army in Korea—how you watched so many men become involved in immorality and become unfaithful to their present or future wives, how you were sickened by their swearing and their vulgar language. You told me that these experiences made you want to teach young people about the commandments of the Lord and to do all you could to help them live lives of honor and love."

"Yes, you are right," I agreed eagerly. "That's what I still want to do. But if I can't teach seminary, then I'll teach those things in my art classes."

With a warning tone in her voice she replied, "You try teaching those things in the public schools and you'll be out of there in a week. You can't teach religion in an art class. Especially an art class in a public school."

"Yes I can," I responded as I walked to the sink for a drink of water. "I won't talk about prayer and the Ten Commandments and stuff like that. But I can do for those young folks what Mr. Brimhall and Mr. Sorensen did for me. I can teach them that somebody cares about them and that they are people of worth. I can help them have confidence. I can help them stand up and become what they ought to be and can be. Oh, Marilyn, I'm not able to explain it the way I'd like to, but in my heart I know I can help the young people who will be in my classes."

"Your job will be to teach them art, not morality."

I was a little frustrated as I tried to explain. "I'll teach them art. But art is one-third talent and two-thirds confidence. Marilyn, I can help them see what they can do not only in art but in life."

Marilyn reached out and took my hand in hers. She looked into my eyes and said, "I think maybe your expectations or dreams are a bit beyond reality, but I can see that you want to be an art teacher, so I sure support you."

Her words sent a surge of happiness through my soul. Almost in tears, I said, "I'm not a great artist now, but I'll keep learning. Someday I'll be the best art teacher in whatever state I'm teaching in."

"What do you mean, whatever state we're in? You mean that we could leave Utah?"

"I don't know. We'll need to go where I can get a job. It's summer now, and so most jobs are gone. But somewhere there is a school that needs a Michelangelo on their faculty. I'll start looking for that place tomorrow."

"When you find the place, tell them they aren't getting just a Michelangelo but also a Peter or a Paul."

I laughed. I knew I was a dreamer. Maybe I wouldn't be able to help all the students look up at the sky the way I wanted, but I'd be able to help some, and I sure was excited to try.

Sensing I had finished expressing my feelings, Marilyn asked, "Are you going to fill out the application form you brought home from your seminary interview?"

"I don't think that would do any good." I remembered again with pain the failed interview.

"Well, it won't do any harm."

"I'll fill it out tomorrow."

Later, as we lay in bed, Marilyn said lovingly, "Good night, Michelangelo—or is it Peter? I guess it's both."

"Good night," I said, chuckling. It had been quite a day. Sleep didn't come quickly. It sometimes doesn't when one tries to live the future before the future comes.

6

Up to the Highest Heights

"D on't you have any friends who can write?" the seminary administrator asked.

I was puzzled. Had he called me back to his office just to ask me such a strange question? I wasn't at all sure what was going on.

During the week since I had begun to try to find a position teaching art, I had without any hope filled out the application to teach seminary. Because the completion of this form required three letters of recommendation, I had asked my former seminary teacher Raymond Bailey, my former stake president Phil Jensen, and my current BYU bishop, Ernest Wilkins, to write these letters.

I didn't know how to respond to his question, so the administrator asked again. "I was just wondering if you had any friends who can write."

Because of his good natured tone and the smile on his face I relaxed a bit and replied, "I'm not sure what you mean."

He chuckled, and said, "What I mean is, the people you asked to write letters of recommendation didn't write. Each one has personally come in here to tell me that I must hire you as a seminary teacher. What do you think of that?"

I had such a feeling of joy that I had to look down and swallow hard to keep some control of my emotions. Then I looked up and said, "I guess they can't write."

He laughed, and then he looked deep into my eyes for a few seconds. His face grew serious as he asked, "Would you be willing to go anywhere we need you if we hire you as a seminary teacher?"

"Anywhere," I replied.

He stood up and came around the desk. I stood and he came to me and extended his hand. As we shook hands he said with enthusiasm, "Welcome aboard!"

A few minutes later I was headed down the hill, but my mind and heart were soaring higher and higher. My broken dream was repaired. I was to be a seminary teacher, but now I knew why. My desire was to teach any subject, so long as I could be involved in helping people find their sky. And now, to teach seminary seemed a special opportunity to do that.

I hurried the several blocks to downtown Provo. Soon I was at the telephone company where Marilyn worked, and with elation I announced to her all that had happened.

I was to be a teacher. The opportunity was there. I couldn't wait to be in my own classroom with my own young students. My dream was coming true.

It's difficult to believe that thirty-five years have passed since I was "welcomed aboard." In that time I have made voyages more exciting than those of Magellan and Columbus. There is no ship that can sail to such places as can the ship of learning and loving and growing. There is no captain aboard any vessel who has so much at his command as I have had as a teacher. No waves are larger, no currents stronger, no doldrums calmer, and no skies bluer than those faced by a teacher.

But, alas, after many years of experience, I still must admit that I really don't know how to teach. If I could write a sure-fire formula on how to teach, it would be by far among the most important formulas ever made.

Although I know but little of how to teach, there are some things that I have learned and do know. Things that seem to be universally true. Things which, on given days and at certain moments, will work. Those things are what I will now focus on.

7

Seeing the Friendly Skies over My New Town

Even though we had all four windows rolled down in our 1947 Chevrolet, it still was uncomfortably hot as Marilyn and I and our young son, Matthew, drove from Provo to Brigham City. Our emotions on that July day were a mixture of excitement and anxiety.

We were excited that my first year as a teacher was to be spent in Brigham City. A week earlier, when the secretary phoned and told me where we were to be assigned, I shouted, "Brigham City! That's where the trees are."

Later, when I told Marilyn, she excitedly exclaimed, "Oh, Brigham City! That's where the trees are."

It was almost as if we felt the trees were more important than the young people who walked and talked and succeeded and failed and dreamed in the shade of those trees.

Our purpose in making this hot summer journey to the city with the tree-lined main street was to purchase a house that we could move into in a month or so. We contacted a real-estate agent. He showed us some beautiful, big houses, but their price tags were far beyond the meager amount we could pay. He showed us some smaller houses, but even they were beyond our budgetary reach.

Finally, in his frustration and our despair, he showed us a teeny tiny house up north of town.

As we walked through the front door it seemed to us that it was the most beautiful house in all of Brigham City. There's an old movie called *The Enchanted Cottage*. A couple who are considered unattractive—he has been disfigured in an accident, while she has simply been deemed plain—move into a cottage. As they live there, something wonderful happens: They become radiantly beautiful to each other. Well, this house didn't suddenly make me handsome, but somehow to Marilyn and me the house itself seemed enchantingly beautiful.

We were pleased to know that if we would give up steak for hamburger, whole milk for powdered milk, and new clothes for old ones, we could just barely meet the monthly house payments.

We purchased that happy house, and in late August we moved inside its walls. We were profoundly happy there. We loved Brigham City. In that fair town was a place called the Peach City Ice Cream Parlor. Every once in a while we'd save enough money to be able to afford a milk shake there. I wouldn't drink such a delicious treat through a straw; instead, I'd tip the big glass and wait for the thick, delicious ice cream to sort of fall in my face. When I'd do that, Marilyn would look away in embarrassment. Some of the girls and guys working at the "Peach City" called me Brother Durrant because—well, because (and I want to say this humbly, even though I was so proud of the fact) I was their seminary teacher.

I remember that as time passed, the bankers of Brigham City, the lawyers, the doctors, the farmers, the plumbers, the policemen—they all came to know me. They called me Brother Durrant. They seemed to consider me a person of importance because I taught their children. I'd see such people at the Peach Day Parade, that festive harvest celebration held the Saturday after Labor Day. As I'd walk along the sidewalk and through the carnival and the art exhibit, people young and old would say, "Hi, Brother Durrant." I'd say hi back, and I'd be happy, because it's good to see people you love.

Brigham City became our town. We planted a lawn and built a white lattice fence for roses to grow up on. We pruned our three front apple trees. We talked to our neighbors, and they became our friends. We loved Brigham City.

The high school was called Box Elder High. Students there were the Box Elder Bees, and a sweeter bunch of bees have never lived. Some of my students played basketball, and some were cheerleaders. They all wanted me to come to their games. Some of the other students weren't good athletes, some weren't popular, and some had troubled foregrounds. But all—the prominent ones and all those who were in the background, the succeeders and those who struggled—all wanted one thing from me. In their own way, they all wanted me to notice them, and I wanted that too.

Marilyn and I didn't have much money in

Brigham City, but there was something I didn't want to tell anyone because I didn't want to make them envious: my family was the richest family in town.

I learned there that if you love the town and the local milk shakes and the parades and ball teams and all sorts of people, and if you plant a lawn and grow red roses and love the young ones, all of life's weather conditions will be favorable. You'll be able to show your students the sky, and nothing makes a teacher and his students happier than that.

8

Through the Dark Clouds Came a Ray of Hope

I'm failing, Brother Horsley," I said to the kind man who was my seminary principal at the Brigham City Seminary. "Those students who just left deserve a better teacher than I'll ever be."

"What happened?" he asked, a look of empathy on his face.

"I don't know. It isn't so much what happened as it is what didn't happen. I just can't get through to that class. Some of my other classes are better, but even in those classes I'm not really doing the job."

Brother Horsley was my friend, and he cared deeply about my success. I sensed that he was glad I had come to Brigham City. He was obviously saddened by my despair.

"Well, I haven't heard any complaints from the students. They seem to like you. A woman told me at church that she sure is glad her son is in your class, because he doesn't like school but he does like seminary."

These words lifted my sagging spirits a little, but I was still hurting as I said, "I guess it isn't what the students or the parents think that matters the most. It's what I think. You see, I have this dream of what I want to do—to teach, to help—but I'm not coming up to that standard. I've wanted a lot of things in life, like popularity and athletic skill, but I've never wanted anything so much as I want to be a good teacher, and, well . . . Brother Horsley, I'm not a good teacher."

"To me you are a good teacher," he said with compassion. "And you're getting better every day."

I almost believed him, but the facts—well, not the facts, but the feelings of the matter—told me there were a million miles to go to get to where I wanted to be, and I wasn't sure I had the ability to get there.

In the mental state I was in at that time I was grateful that the Christmas break was upon us. That signaled the near halfway mark of my first year. Maybe after nearly two weeks off I'd be able to muster the courage to keep going and, I hoped, keep growing.

We got out of school on Tuesday, and Christmas wasn't until Thursday. That Tuesday night I drove to the seminary building. It was seven-thirty in the evening, two days before Christmas. Brother Horsley had told me I could take my classroom Christmas tree home if I desired, so I had come to pick it up. That would save us a few dollars that we could spend on other Christmas needs.

As I entered my classroom and switched on the lights, my eyes fell on the thirty-six empty seats. It was strangely quiet, and the room suddenly seemed sacred. I plugged in the Christmas tree lights and walked near the blackboard where I had so often stood facing the students. I looked out at the empty seats and envisioned my students sitting there, looking up at me with "please teach me" expressions on their faces. Tears filled my eyes as I beheld them. Somehow, in just seconds I thought of them not as a group but as individuals. I could see the sky that was part of each one.

There was something wonderful about being there alone in that building. I felt inclined to kneel, and as I did I realized that I knelt on sacred ground.

As I prayed I recalled the students who troubled me most and made me feel like such a failure. I remembered past lessons, some of which hadn't worked. But then my mind was flooded with memories of successes. An overwhelming feeling of love came into my soul, and a comforting influence told me that all was well.

I prayed that what I had done in that classroom would be of some import to my dear friends who had so often met with me there. And I prayed for success during the remainder of the year.

I arose from my knees, put on a Christmas record, and began to undecorate the tree. Usually, plucking ornaments from the green boughs saddens me, but not this time. I could hear the words "O holy night" coming from the phonograph, and I knew what those words meant. As I dragged the tree from the room and switched out the light, I knew that Brother Horsley was right when he said to me, "You are a good teacher, and you're getting better every day."

Yes indeed, I would get better—not better than others, but better than I'd ever been before. The thought of not being where I wanted to be in my teaching ability was no longer a cause for discouragement or for a desire to jump ship. Instead, the thought of the distance I had to go excited and challenged me.

The teaching ocean was vast, but I was ready to set sail right into the middle of it, and, by George, I'd make it to my longed-for shore.

Since that time I've learned that teaching can be the most discouraging of all activities, but it can also be the most uplifting.

A teaching colleague of mine told me of this experience. He saw another colleague, Donl Peterson, coming down the hall and asked him, "How are you doing?" Donl replied, "I just was in the most magnificent class I've ever been in." My colleague asked, "Oh really? Who was teaching it?" Donl replied, "I was."

A week later the two met again. This time Donl said, "I was just in the worst class I've ever been in." "Oh really?" My colleague asked. "Who was the teacher?" "I was," replied a downcast Donl.

So it is with teaching. It can lift you to the highest heaven or lower you to a form of . . . well, quite the opposite of heaven. And if it doesn't do those things to you and me as we teach, it is because we don't care. Good teachers must care. With a prayerful desire they must want to cause something wonderful to happen to the hearts and minds of the learners. If all effort seems shallow and empty, or if the students aren't receptive, then emotional pain must register in the teacher's heart.

But if things so fervently desired do occur, then oh, the indescribable joy that comes to a teacher's heart!

I get excited as I write this. I want to run to the classroom and try to make it happen. That eagerness and the hoped-for results and the once-in-a-while success are why teaching is so godly an act.

9

Skying High One-on-One

Y ou've got to win by two," I shouted as my more-than-worthy opponent scored on a lucky hook shot from the left side of the basket. It had been a grueling game to this point. We matched basket after basket. I was putting all I had into defense, and I knew that I must score on each possession or he'd win. The thought of his winning, more than my losing, gave me supreme motivation, for if he won I would have let down all the students. I was in my last year of high school, and going down to defeat at the hands of a teacher—worse yet, a student teacher—was inexcusable. It would have disgraced the entire senior class.

After the teacher scored, he personally delivered the ball to me where the top of the key would have been painted had we not been playing on a dirt court at a campground. As he handed me the ball he crouched down in a defensive stance, and we looked deeply into each other's eyes with determination that defied description.

Suddenly I faked right, but he stayed firm. I went left, and quickly he was directly in my way. I knew my only hope was to jump and shoot. The ball was on line. If it went in, we'd be tied. I could tell he was tired by the way he was gasping for breath. I knew that if I could tie it now, I'd win.

Just as I celebrated in my mind, the ball hit the back of the rim and catapulted back toward me. I had to get the rebound, but it was just a fraction of an inch beyond my grasp. He had it.

I pressed him as closely as I could without fouling. He was breathing so hard I knew his accuracy on a long shot would be poor. I knew I must not let him get around me.

Suddenly he jumped and shot. The ball, to my relief, was way off course. I moved quickly to get the rebound. But there was no rebound. The ball careened off the old wooden backboard through the hoop. It was over. He had won.

He gasped, and then said, "Good job, George"—gasp—"you're a"—gasp—"good player."

The other students mumbled their disapproval of my performance as they headed to get their barbecued hamburgers. The lines for the food were long. Seeing that we would be last, my opponent and I sat down on a log near the creek and began to talk. First we spoke of where he went to high school and about the time he played varsity basketball. After several minutes of conversation, I asked him where he would be teaching seminary the next year. I was shocked at his reply.

He picked a stick up from the ground and, holding it in his right hand, tapped it gently into his left. I could tell he was in deep thought. Finally he spoke. "I was thinking about that today. You know, while I've been teaching your class, things haven't gone so well. I can't seem to keep you guys interested. I can tell you've personally been bored, because you spend most of your time sitting in the back talking to Val and Bob."

He was hitting his hand harder now as he continued, "I guess I'm just not cut out to be a teacher. So my wife and I decided today that I'd go into business with my brother."

He fell silent. I couldn't respond—it never occurred to me that he wouldn't be a teacher. To me he was the best there was. I could tell from the first day he came to our classroom that he liked me. He liked all of us. *Maybe that's why we took advantage of him,* I thought.

"Don't quit being a teacher," I pleaded. "You're the first teacher who ever played me one-on-one. I love your class. I know I talk a lot, but that doesn't mean I'm not listening." As we walked toward the food line I said, "I'm sorry. It's just—well, anyway, I like you. Don't quit." At that point someone called us to come eat, and so our talk ended.

But he did quit, this wonderful man whom I remember now some forty-five years later. A man whom I now recognize was a role model gave up teaching to go into business, and a lunkhead like me helped him to decide that. I'm not writing to criticize myself. I'm writing on behalf of all the lunkheads and all the duds (and I'm addressing myself) to you who could be great teachers. Don't quit because of supposed failure. We mature, we creatures who, as Christ's words indicate, need to be taught that we can be good human beings. Don't quit; we need you. Don't turn away. Not for money nor for an easier way. You know who you are. You feel it in your heart that you should be a teacher. Don't turn your back on us; don't turn your back on teaching.

If you do follow another dream as far as what you'll do for a living, be sure to let teaching be your fondest avocation.

You men, teach the little ones, teach the Scouts in all their varieties. Teach the deacons to tie ties and to pass the sacrament. Teach the priests—the wonderful priests, who are halfway to nowhere or somewhere—and show them the sky. Teach the prospective missionaries; teach those glorious early-morning seminarians who arise from their beds willingly or unwillingly while night has not yet departed.

You women, teach the Primary children, the Beehives, the Mia Maids, and the Laurels to be what God desires them to be. Help them know that virtue is indeed its own reward. Teach the sisters in Relief Society how good life can be if they'll look at the sky. Teach the students in early-morning seminary that sacrifice brings forth blessings.

I know I have listed but a small portion of the opportunities that will come to you as you are called to teach.

So many of my most memorable experiences have come as a result of my calling as a teacher, rather than my profession as a teacher.

You asked: "What happened to the teacher who played you one-on-one?"

Well, because rumors spread fast about his beating me, he was taken in the first round of the NBA draft. No, no, I'm just kidding.

I don't know what happened to him. I never saw him again after that year.

I imagine he probably did well in business. But while he pursued that vocation, I hope he played a lot of young men like me "one-on-one." After all, teaching, if it were reported on the sports page, would almost always be reported as "one-on-one." I hope he taught the seventeen-year-olds in a Sunday school class and went one-on-one with a young man who was struggling with a Word of Wisdom problem. I hope he taught a young lady who was suffering from lack of hope, lack of social life, and lack of self-worth, and helped her look up and win.

I hope he has been a bishop and has gone one-on-one in his office with a scoutmaster who wanted to quit, and persuaded him to hang in there. I hope he has helped a young father to turn back to his family and away from the world.

Oh, I have so many hopes for him. He's out there somewhere. If you see him, thank him for me and tell him he helped me see the sky. Tell him to get on his playing shoes and I'll thrash him "one-on-one."

10

Many Ways, but Only One Way

When I set out to write this book, I was filled with confidence that I had many specific suggestions on how to be a good teacher. But now with the task at hand, my confidence has abandoned me.

I had hoped to say to you, "This is what I do, and it works for me. So you listen to my magnificent ideas, and surely you'll be a success." But then I thought of you and how you teach, and I realized it was you and not me who should be writing this book, for it is you who is more successful than me. I'm not putting myself down, for I do all right, but it is you who so often makes me long to teach as you do.

So here is the pen; you write the book. Well, go ahead. What are you waiting for? Yes, it is hard, but you can do it. I can't, but you can. Go ahead.

Forgive me for pushing you. You'll need time to think. And I assure you, the more you think, the more frustrated you will become. Finally, you'll have to fall back on personal incidents that have helped you.

For example, I could say, Here's a surefire way to be a successful teacher: Tell the class members of your personal experiences. Tell them about when you were their age and you were living in American Fork. Tell the exciting things you did then. Using that approach works for me.

But then I don't suppose you lived in American Fork, did you? So I guess that idea won't work for you.

I could advise you to speak of the struggles you had as you grew up. Tell how difficult it was for you to develop a good personality because you always were able to get by on your looks. The way I did.

But of course, perhaps you were not so handsome as I. And so that idea doesn't apply.

Next I could suggest that you use a liberal dose of humor in all your teaching presentations.

But you'd likely reply, "How can I be as funny as you if I don't look as funny as you?"

All right, then. Use the blackboard. Draw illustrations of what you are saying. That works for me.

You'd throw your arms in the air and the chalk would fly from your hand as you would exclaim, "But I can't even draw a straight line."

Well, then speak about sports to the young folks. They love sports. Tell them, as I do, how I started three years in a row for my ward team and finally made all-stake.

You'd reply, "But I was all-state, and to give an accurate description of my sports career would sound as though I'm bragging."

Okay, then talk of being shy and not being able to get up the confidence to ask a girl for a date. Young people like those kinds of stories, because many of them are shy.

"No," you'd say, "I don't like to get personal like that. My personal life is my business, and I don't intend to share it."

I'd suggest to keep things simple so that all can succeed. Make your students work, but not so hard that they suffer from continued stress.

You'd reply, "I'm not concerned with their stress. I'm going to make them work harder than they've ever worked before. My students will be prepared for the real world when they get out of my class."

Be sure to show them how to apply what they've learned. That gives the learning real relevance and holds their interest.

You'd answer, "Hey! I'll teach them the facts, and they can learn to apply them on their own."

I'd come to understand that you and I are really quite different. Because I feel so strongly about the way I do things, I'd be amazed that even though you do things differently, you are very successful.

Then I'd know that there is more than one way to teach. Maybe even more than one hundred ways.

So should we throw in the towel on this book and acknowledge that there is no way to tell others how to teach? Or should we get back to the most basic fundamentals of teaching and see if there is common ground there? I mean, should we compare teaching to a tree and go back beyond the leaves of the teacher's personality and the limbs of teaching methods, and go right down through the trunk of subject matter and get deep down into the ground and look at the very roots of teaching?

These roots, if tapped into, would be a sure foundation for success. That is what I've decided to do after much almost-painful consideration of what the roots might be. I heard in my mind the words, "Charity never faileth."

"Never faileth"! That is quite a guarantee. I know that new math might fail or be replaced by newer math, and that phonics could become as outdated as the Phoenicians, and that many teaching techniques might someday be as obsolete to schools as the practice of bleeding is to medicine.

So I turned to one of the world's greatest teachers, the one who said, "Charity never faileth." Yes, I turned to Mr. Paul, who taught at Corinth High School and whose lesson number 13 describes the roots of teaching—the very roots of what makes a good teacher great, and a great teacher a master teacher.

In his message to teachers and students everywhere, Mr. Paul states: "Though I speak with the tongues of men and of angels, and have not charity, I am become as sounding brass, or a tinkling cymbal."

What does that bring to your mind about teaching? I can think of nothing that would devastate me more than if a student said to me, "Mr. Durrant, you sure can say things well, and you really know the facts, but somehow there is something about you that just doesn't ring true."

Well! Considering how Mr. Paul's opening words get right at a problem that can devastate good teaching, I wonder how he proposes that you and I make sure we do ring true.

In the next chapters we will consider Mr. Paul's solution to the problem he poses. Let's turn now to the rest of the story.

11

Only Through Charity Can We Reveal the Sky

I sat with a new teacher in an area faculty meeting. A very entertaining instructor was giving seven ways in which he felt we could improve as teachers. His points were sound and made with clarity; for that reason I was a bit surprised when my associate whispered to me, "He thinks he is so clever."

I hadn't sensed what my colleague felt, but I'll never forget what I learned from his perception. I determined then and there that as a teacher I would try with all I possessed to never rely on cleverness or on deliberately pulling certain strings to draw certain reactions from those I taught.

Now, I know that at times I myself will appear to some as an entertainer or as one who goes for predetermined spiritual or intellectual punch lines. But I try—oh, how I try—to avoid that.

Paul got at what I'm trying to say when he said: "And though I have the gift of prophecy [or, perhaps, the gift of ably presenting subject matter], and understand all mysteries, and all knowledge [or understand the subject matter almost perfectly]; and though I have all faith, so that I could remove mountains [or am confident of being an expert in the field], and have not charity, I am nothing" (1 Corinthians 13:2).

So there it is, the first principle of life and teaching: Charity. The underlying prompting motive, without which everything else adds up to nothing.

When charity is present in our hearts as teachers, then it pushes all cleverness, all manipulation, and all unrighteous dominion aside and allows us to teach so that what we feel and say rings true. If charity isn't at the foundation of our thoughts, then our words will indeed be as sounding brass or a tinkling cymbal.

It's difficult to define charity. To me, figuratively speaking it has much to do with overlooking all outward appearances and seeing the glorious sky in the souls of others, and helping them see in themselves what we can see in them. It means looking beyond the foregrounds that so often disguise those we teach, that make them seem hardened or damaged, noncaring or boastful, unmotivated or vulgar, or manipulative, or beyond reach. It means to look upon the pure blue sky of their unclouded hearts.

It involves not only seeing the students that way but also seeing the school where we teach, the administrators who lead us, our teaching colleagues, and our community in the same light. To see our spouse and our children that way and, most of all, to see ourselves that way is indeed to look at the sky.

Then and only then can we nourish or, if necessary, help ourselves and others rearrange, repaint, and refurbish our foreground to be as beautiful as our sky.

Knowing that Paul is right, just imagine what we could do as teachers if we took our ability to present our message excellently, our almost perfect knowledge of our subject matter, and our confidence in our ability to reach the minds and hearts of the students and then pushed all these things a bit up off the ground so that we could make room for a foundation of charity. Then we would let all else rest firmly on charity. And then, my friends, my fellow teachers—then, instead of being nothing, you and I and all teachers could really be something.

But *how?* That's the big question. How can we have a foundation of charity that will enable us to look at the sky?

Let's see how Mr. Paul answers that question. He said that if we have charity we will

—be willing to suffer long
—be kind
—envy not
—not vaunt ourselves or be puffed up
—not behave ourselves unseemly
—seek not our own
—be not easily provoked
—think no evil
—rejoice not in iniquity but in truth
—believe all things

If Paul were here and we said to him, "So is that it, Paul? If we do the things you listed, will we have charity and thus ring true in all we say and do?"

Paul might say, "Well, there is more to it than that, but if you do those things on the list—or at least have a burning desire to do them—then, if you pray for charity with all the energy of heart, you'll feel charity, and when you do you'll really be something."

Then will we be master teachers, Mr. Paul? "Yes, indeed, you will. But often it will be a private thing, and only your students, one or two at a time, will know. In certain sacred moments you and those you teach will understand each other, and you'll be edified and rejoice together—or, as you are saying, both you and your students will see the sky. When that happens, then you will be a teacher."

Now let's look more specifically at the principles that will lead to the guaranteed success of which Mr. Paul spoke.

12

Only the Teacher Knows

It was about the scariest day of my life when Ken Sheffield came to visit my classes. Brother Sheffield was the supervisor of all the seminaries in northern Utah, and there wasn't a finer man on the earth. He was coming to observe me teach and to evaluate my effectiveness. He would compare me to all the other teachers and rate me as an A, B, or C teacher.

I knew he would be fair, and that was what made me nervous.

Because he would visit five other teachers at the Brigham City seminary, he would come to only one of my five classes, and I didn't know just when he'd walk in. He didn't come first period or second, and my anxiety increased with each passing moment.

Then, as the last of my second-period students disappeared out the doorway, my heart leaped up into my throat as all five feet four inches of Brother Sheffield entered my room. My time had come.

Before I could arise from my desk at the front of the classroom, this exuberant man hurried to me. With great gusto he took my hand in his and, while shaking my hand vigorously, announced, "Brother Durrant, I hear that you're doing a fine job in your first year of teaching. Do you mind if I just sit in the back and watch and see how you do it?"

"Sure, Brother Sheffield. Thanks for coming," I answered, almost sincerely.

Class began. The students sang quite well. Ryan read a scripture, and for the first time he didn't laugh as he read it. Annette prayed in her usual "personal conversation with God" style.

We were off to a good start, and I was beginning to breathe in an almost normal manner.

After the opening prayer was concluded, I arose and complimented the class members, especially Ryan and Annette. I then announced: "As you know, our test is tomorrow, so today we will have a review. To do that we'll divide into five teams and play a little competitive game."

I assigned each student to a team. Now we were ready. I said, "All right, team number one and student number one on that team—let's see, that would be you, Fred—this question goes to you. Who was the man who left Ur and went to Haran?"

"Abraham! Abraham!" Fred shouted with glee.

"Right!" I said approvingly as I recorded a mark on the blackboard next to where I had written "Team Number One." As I did so, all those on that team busily congratulated Fred.

"Now team two and student one. Patrick. Only Patrick can answer. Patrick, who was Abraham's father?"

Patrick squirmed in his seat with nervousness. After a pause he said, "Lot. It was Lot."

"Is that right, team three?" I asked.

"No, no," they shouted.

"Then Van—you are the first one on team three—who was it?"

"Terah."

"Right!" I said. "Good work, Van. That was a hard one—that's why even Patrick, who's an Old Testament scholar, missed it. He'll likely never miss another question. And now, team three, you can get an extra point if you answer your regular question correctly."

The class interest was much more intense than I had expected. Problems that I had on a daily basis with that class didn't come up that day. I glanced at Brother Sheffield from time to time, and I could see that he was enthusiastically enjoying what was going on.

The class ended, and the students, in a quiet and orderly (and, I might say, uncharacteristic) manner, departed.

"Oh, my," Brother Sheffield said. "That was real teaching!" He repeated, "That was real teaching!"

I was exhilarated as he confirmed what I sensed had been a far better experience than I had expected.

"Thank you, Brother Sheffield. I think your being there helped us all to do better. Will you come back to my next class?"

"Oh, no, I've seen enough. I know an A teacher when I see one."

That night I phoned Brother Sheffield at home, and, as nearly as I can recall, I said, "Brother Sheffield, I believe I misled you today. I made you think I'm an A teacher, and, Brother Sheffield, I'm not. I don't know what happened in that classroom while you were there today; the class usually isn't like that. Usually some students aren't interested, and I can't hold their attention. Often I lose track, or at least I lose the strength of what I want to say. I could go on, Brother Sheffield, but I hope you understand. I'm not an A teacher. If you could be generous enough to rate me at a B, that would be where I am sometimes when I'm not a C.

This wonderful man did not respond for several seconds. Then he softly said, "All right, I'll rate you as a B. That will give you a challenge to do even better next year."

After I hung up, I felt sorry I had called. It would have been such an honor to be an A. *Maybe I'm too hard on myself,* I thought. *Maybe I am an A teacher.* But then I remembered my total teaching experience that year. I remembered thinking that I alone knew as a teacher what went on in my private classroom. When I considered that, I felt better. There were times I was an A, but most of the time I was a B. Then I shuddered as I realized that on any given day, at least for a few minutes, Brother Sheffield would have caught a glimpse of a real C.

Thus, I learned something that those of you who teach also know: When visitors come to our classes they have no way to see things as they are. Their very presence adds an ingredient that changes the mix. Some teachers (and I believe I'm one of these) can perform well when they're being observed. Others lose their edge of excellence when the nervousness caused by a visitor enters their hearts.

So, knowing this, who can evaluate my teaching effectiveness? The answer is, I can. Because I'm always there. I know what goes on minute by minute and day by day. But, of course, some of us are quite hard on ourselves and put ourselves down. Others are so defensive that instead of seeking a better way of teaching, they almost deceive themselves into thinking they are A's even though no one else, including the students, would agree.

For those of us who really are B's but long to be A's, how can we—not in the eyes of others, but in our own eyes—make the exalting step up? The answer, of course, along with expertly teaching sound subject matter, is to do something that never fails. As Paul said, we must have charity. We must not leave excellent teaching undone. Excellent teaching alone won't get us up to an A, but such teaching, plus charity, can take us all the way to the sky.

13

In the Midst of Long-Suffering, There Was the Sky

During my second year in Brigham City, in the early part of the winter, my dear friend Brother Horsley suddenly became ill. Two days later, he died. This great man had had many moments in which he was a master teacher. He could control rowdy students in a most effective manner. Meeting the needs of one rambunctious class required every one of his special skills. All of us on the faculty, knowing the makeup of this group, marveled that Brother Horsley was succeeding with them.

But now Brother Horsley was gone, and each of us agreed to teach one of his classes so that hiring a new teacher wouldn't be necessary.

What I feared most happened. I was free fifth period, and that was when the infamous class met.

Brother Bowen, the newly appointed principal, gulped as he said, "George, you've been teaching the ninth graders, but now I see no choice but to invite you to step in and teach Brother Horsley's fifth period." He paused as if in pain for me, then continued, "Brother Horsley's fine class of juniors and seniors."

I knew I was about to "suffer long," not by choice, but by decree.

The next day I recalled a story I'd heard another teacher tell. He'd said, "When one of my classes would come over to the seminary from the high school, I'd watch them approach, and I'd be reminded of what Delilah told Samson. I'd say to myself, 'The Philistines are upon us.'"

It was fifth hour. I said good-bye to my fourth-hour ninth graders and walked the fifteen steps to the door of Brother Horsley's room. I paused, took a deep breath, and entered. My suffering was about to begin.

My anticipation of suffering was not an underestimate. I did indeed suffer or struggle much during those fateful four months, but amid the suffering, as is always the case, I experienced much joy. Now, strangely, after many years have passed, about all I remember is the joy.

Thinking back, I recall that during the first several days with this class I had determined to be tough and not to allow a single ounce of tomfoolery. But these students knew what tough was, and they could tell that I wasn't it. Early confrontations with them did nothing more than cause me to lose all semblance of charity, and at the same time, my attitude and behavior caused them to be more determined than ever to destroy any environment in which positive learning could occur.,

In frustration I decided that by all indications I

was losing. Having acknowledged that dismal truth, an idea entered my head, and I said to myself, *I can't conquer them, so I'll join them.*

Carrying out this new strategy, I'd reason with them about what was taking place in our class. We talked of why we needed things to change. I recall that one day, right after our song, prayer, and scripture, my heart was sick because they had mockingly carried out these sacred activities.

I told them of my deep disappointment and announced that thereafter we would not have a devotional at the beginning of class. I sincerely reasoned that such sacred things as prayer and scripture reading could not be done in a light-minded manner without in a sense mocking God.

The largest fellow in the class, who was nicknamed "Mr. Clean," objected, stating, "Come on, Brother Durrant. Don't make us stop having devotionals. We want to have a devotional."

I answered, "So do I. I want to have a devotional with all my heart. But we can't because we can't be reverent, and so we won't."

The big fellow said, "What do you mean, we can't be reverent? We can be more reverent than those little ninth graders that you love so much."

"Yeah," chimed in two or three others. "We can be reverent. You just let us have a devotional tomorrow, and we'll show you reverent."

And so they did. I didn't set out to be a master teacher at that moment. But I loved them, and when I told them about the need for reverence they sensed that I was sincere (not as sounding brass), and they felt that what I was saying was true. At that moment, we rejoiced together.

That wasn't the end of the battle, but we all were now going the same direction. The confrontations were no longer with the entire class, just with some individuals.

One fellow who sat on the front row was the greatest troublemaker of them all. He disrupted almost continually with his lightminded remarks. But to my delight, I learned that if I would move to the other side of the room and speak in a low volume, he would soon drift off to sleep. With him asleep, the class could move forward in a more effective manner.

When the bell would ring, signaling that class was over, I'd wake that student up and the two of us would walk together to the front door of the seminary building. One day as we walked, he told me that he worked at a job every night until two in the morning. I told him how hard it would be for me to stay awake if I went to bed as late as he did. I thanked him for coming to class so faithfully. He could see that I understood, and as time passed, he and I became good friends.

Each day at the end of class I would wake him up as gently and respectfully as I could and then walk to the door with him. He could tell that I liked him, because it's hard to hide something like that. Each day, as we walked to the door together, I had a few moments when I was a master teacher.

As my students and I talked in that fifth hour class, we often got off the subject. The students liked to talk about sports and polygamy and who is sealed to whom when there is a divorce and the army and college life.

If someone had come in and seen the casual manner of things, I'm sure they would have said, "Poor Brother Durrant. He can't handle those big guys. They know how to make him suffer. He's a good guy, but he's a C teacher at best."

They would have been right. But I knew then of the private moments and the feelings that I shared with those "rowdy ones." They sort of reminded me of when I was a younger me. Perhaps because of that I had a genuine love for them, and that made it so I could see beyond their foreground. I could see their sky. In a way I often said to each of them, "See up there, way up there? That's you up there." And I'd know that they could see what I'd see. In the months that followed, many of them asked me to speak at their missionary farewells.

Oh, how I loved them. Amid my suffering as a C teacher, I had some masterful moments of true teaching.

14

Being Kind Lifts Eyes to the Sky

One thing that can make me more "easily provoked" is to not get enough sleep.

My idea of a perfect evening is to watch the ten o'clock news and then, right after the last sports score, go to bed.

But Glen didn't know that. He didn't know how irritated I was when, each night for four nights in a row at about 10:10, he'd knock on my door and ask if we could talk.

I would reluctantly turn off the TV, and we'd talk. I should say, he would talk. I wouldn't speak much, in the hopes that he would run out of things to say and go home so I'd be able to go to bed.

Glen was struggling at that time in his life. He had an intense desire to be good, and he had little tolerance for those who didn't share his lofty standards.

I can recall his saying: "Brother Durrant, you're a nice guy, and you treat everyone in your class real well. But if you knew what I know you would change, because you see, Brother Durrant, some of the guys in the class are no good."

I just listened. He continued: "You see them in class, and they're all goody-goody there. But you ought to see them in the locker room over at the high school. They don't care what they say over there. They're like a bunch of animals."

I didn't respond, even though I felt he was overstating the problems of his associates.

After a pause he added: "You know when we have the devotional in our class—I don't know if you've noticed, but I close my eyes not just during the prayer but also during the spiritual thought and even the song. Do you know why I do that, Brother Durrant?"

I replied, "I have noticed that. Why do you do that?"

"Because when we're having our devotional, we are worshipping God. And when we are worshipping God, I don't want to look around at a bunch of guys who mock God and who are all going to hell."

Glen had tears welling up in his eyes as he finished his heartfelt statement.

I was inclined to give him a speech on self-righteousness or on not judging. I almost told him, "They're not as bad as you imagine," but I just said, "I understand, Glen. I understand."

A few minutes later he was gone, and I was kneeling and asking the Lord to bless my friend Glen.

Glen and I talked a lot. He often almost irritated me because he took much of my time when I needed to be doing other pressing things. But at the same time I, at least on the outside, was kind to him.

Maybe one of the greatest of all kindnesses is to listen and to pay attention to those who can be a bit irritating.

A few weeks later, during our devotional, I saw that Glen kept his eyes closed during the prayer. At least, I think he did. But his eyes were wide open during the scripture. While we were singing I looked over at him, and a smile crossed his face as his eyes met mine.

That night at 10:10, as he had so often done, Glen knocked on my door. "Brother Durrant," he said happily, "I can't come in. But I just came by to thank you. By talking to me the last few weeks, you've helped me understand that the other guys in the class aren't so bad. Oh, they've got problems, but I do too. So now I like looking around at them when we're worshipping God, because I love them. Thanks, Brother Durrant, for teaching me to open my eyes."

Before I could respond, he turned and bounded down the front steps. Then he was gone. As I lay in bed that night, I tried to think of what it was that I had said to Glen to help him open his eyes. I couldn't think of anything I had said to him about anything. I went to sleep, still unable to recall my wonderful words of wisdom.

It's easy to be kind when it's easy to be kind. But it's hard to be kind when it's hard to be kind. All kindnesses count, but the ones that count most are the kindnesses you give when it's hard to be kind.

Some students, usually one or two or several in every class, are of an irritating variety. Those are the ones to really be kind to. Some will cling to you if you are kind. They stick around after school and keep you from other things like preparation for tomorrow's classes. That's all right, because the greatest preparation for tomorrow is today's kindnesses. The feelings that kindnesses bring today are the feelings that make tomorrow's sky a bit more beautiful.

Sometimes we are so caught up in rules and assignment due dates that when a student desires an exception, we refuse. Sometimes such an exception could make a profound difference. The balance of judgment between justice and mercy faces the teacher each day. Some need justice, but at times, mercy is the answer. What should we do if in doubt? Someone wisely said, "When in doubt, do the kind thing."

Lift people by kind words, by listening, by giving them your time. Listen to the pleading of those who silently say, "Please don't shoot me down. I'm quite capable of crashing on my own."

Help them avoid crashing by being a little more kind. Kindness can bring the sky right down into the foreground.

15

Being Easily Provoked Causes a Downward View

On January 23, 1959, the world stopped turning, and all human activity came to a halt, for on that day the eyes of all mankind focused on my classroom in Brigham City, Utah.

For you see, that was the day I was teaching the seventh of the Ten Commandments. Yes, that was the day that I taught some 150 ninth graders about the law of chastity.

On that fateful day I thought that all the billions of people on earth sensed that if I did not reach the heart of each student, the world would never recover.

I had taught important ideas before, and many times since I have taught on subjects of profound importance. But never have I felt so compelled to succeed in reaching my students as I did that day.

The day before I was to change 150 hearts I had sought wisdom from the other teachers on how to address these vital matters.

"How do you teach such a delicate and sensitive subject?" I asked.

"It's not easy," said one, "but just be frank and tell them the way it is."

Another counseled, "Don't be very specific, or you could get in trouble."

A third advised, "Talk about the joy of marriage and of having children. Keep it positive, and help them desire to live the law of chastity."

The advice helped, but I was so uncertain.

I had taught the commandment "Thou shalt not kill" with some degree of effectiveness and felt quite certain that none of my students would kill each other during the rest of the school year, and likely never. So I felt successful.

When I taught of honoring parents I told of my father and mother. I got carried away as I thought of my mother and how I used to kiss her good-night and tell her I loved her. I felt inspired to assign them to tell their mothers that night, "I love you, Mother."

One girl cried as I taught of loving one's parents. Her father was critically ill in the hospital and had little chance to live. Others seemed touched by my message, and I sensed I had reached their hearts. But one big fellow laughed when I asked him if he would tell his mom he loved her. He told me he thought my assignment was dumb. I felt a brief feeling of failure and wondered if such an assignment was appropriate, but I knew that all in all I had taught well of honoring parents.

Somehow, teaching about parents and not killing had not caused me concern. But teaching these dear young friends about something so delicate as the law of chastity caused me to feel pressure I'd never before known as a teacher.

As I retired the night before I was to teach, I knelt at my bedside and earnestly prayed that I would be able to teach in such a way that these young folks would forever live this supreme commandment.

The next morning I awoke before it was time to arise. I wanted more sleep, but I was too keyed up.

As I entered the seminary building I could scarcely say hello to the other teachers. My mind was too consumed by my intense desire to succeed. I did indeed feel that the world had stopped to watch to see if I could plant these seeds of truth in the hearts of my 150 students.

When the twenty-nine who made up my first-hour class came in they seemed noisier than I'd ever seen them. I sternly advised them to settle down. Most did, but two girls kept talking to each other. I was slightly irritated with them. As the class progressed, I felt I was making the points I desired to make. But the restlessness of several students caused me to wonder why they couldn't see that what I was telling them was the most important thing they had heard or would ever hear. At times my mind was more focused on their immature behavior than it was on my message.

I must say, I was quite annoyed with them—especially the two girls who I felt needed this message most but who continued to want to talk to each other.

My next three classes were a bit better, but still I knew the impact of my message wasn't there. I was saying things from my head, but my own heart was not in it. That made me try to force it by being more firm in my tone and more serious in my expression. I felt I must muster the power to reach them. But the harder I tried, the more I noticed some were slumping in their chairs while others were looking out the window. One was doing homework for another class.

I soon passed beyond feelings of irritation, and I was now deeply annoyed. Certainly the fact that my message wasn't getting through was not my fault; it was the fault of the young people who didn't have the sense to know that what I was saying could make or break their very lives.

As my last class walked in, I almost dreaded their presence. But I took a deep breath and vowed that this hour I would gain the result I had so longed for. This time I would pray for the power to teach. This time I would speak with conviction. This time I would insist on reverent behavior.

The first few minutes went well. I was doing better, and most were listening. Only Richard was causing any problems. I said with some irritation, "Richard, could you please pay attention and stop pestering Jennie."

A minute later, just as I said something that was dear to my heart, Richard laughed.

I quickly left my place at the front of the class and was at his side. As I looked down I said sternly, "Richard, since you think everything is so funny, maybe you'd think it was funny if you got up and left."

He sat there silently. But I persisted. "Did you hear me? I don't want you in here; this isn't the first time you've caused problems. I've talked to you before. I'm tired of it. I don't want you in here anymore. You get up and go over to the counselor and tell him you need another class."

He was in the ninth grade, just a little guy. It breaks my heart now as I can see him get up, and without looking back, he was gone.

The other teachers learned of what I'd done,

and they told me they understood. They added that we couldn't let one student destroy a whole class. The school counselor told me that Richard had been dismissed from two other classes. So I was vindicated. I probably had taught him a lesson that would be good for him.

But now, and even then, even that night, even that moment, I knew I was so very wrong.

You might disagree and say, "Come on, George, get real. Sometimes if you are provoked, you have to take a stand. You can put up with some nonsense, but finally someone has to go."

Maybe so.

But that day. That day when I felt so much pressure to teach so well. That day when I was so overwhelmed with my role as a teacher. That day when my message was so much more important in my mind than was little old Richard. That was not my best moment as a teacher.

Perhaps the reason the story of Richard has been so painful for me to recall is that the experience was so unlike me.

I may not be good at everything Paul spoke of, but I'm really not easily provoked. It takes a lot to provoke me. I sometimes wish I were better at getting provoked. After all, Paul didn't say, "Don't get provoked"—he knew that some behavior, when taken to a certain degree, ought to provoke us. But little things and immature behavior should not easily provoke us teachers.

One of the easiest things in all the world is to provoke some teachers. One little remark by a student can do it, and some students take great glee in provoking an easily provoked teacher. By being too easily provoked, teachers can have a rule of semi-terror in their classrooms.

Oh, the joy of students when they are privileged to be in the classroom with a teacher who is not easily provoked, one whom they respect, not out of fear of his or her rage but out of basking in the teacher's love. A teacher who, when things begin to get out of hand, may say, with some degree of provocation, "All right, that's enough. Settle down."

By limiting the times we are provoked to just once in a while—and then not because of pressure or personal problems, but because of continued misbehavior—we can help set a tone in a classroom wherein you and I can have some masterful moments of pure teaching.

Some might say, "I don't want to be easily provoked, but I can't help it. What can I do?" To such people I might respond, "I find help in remembering how provoking I once was as a young person, and that gives me more patience." But if you had no such problems, then that won't work for you.

It might help to make a commitment each day such as, "Today I will not be easily provoked. I will act as if I do not see nor hear the little things students do that provoke me. I will maintain my sense of humor, because although the students are wonderful, and I take their needs seriously too, they really are quite funny."

Also remember that you yourself, although a masterful teacher, are a little funny. And you are really funny when you frequently make mountains out of molehills.

Most of all, pray for the ability to be consistent. Don't be totally pleasant one day and thoroughly irritable the next. If you have dark feelings, don't take them out on the students.

Say to yourself often, *What an honor it is to be here with these young folks!* Many have foregrounds that are in slight disarray, and some are really all messed up, but in my better moments I sense that each one has a beautiful sky. Look at the sky, and it will cut your provocations by 67 percent.

And now, Richard, wherever you are, I hope you are all right. If it means anything to you, I love you, and I'm sorry.

16

Vaunting Oneself Blocks the View of the Sky

As I said earlier, I was happy to be assigned to Brigham City to begin my teaching career. The only fly in the ointment was that each day after the regular school day at Box Elder High School, I was assigned to go across town to teach the young Navajos who attended seminary at the Intermountain Indian School after their regular school day ended.

At the first of the school year I saw little good that would come to me in my "Indian" assignment. My happiness, I then supposed, would come as I taught and related to the "regular" students. Leaving Box Elder High right after school would take me away from students who would come to the seminary to work on special projects and to visit. I wouldn't be able to go over to the high school to watch athletic practices. So because of my undesirable assignment, many of my associations with the public school students would be stymied. Besides that, teaching the Navajo students would not intellectually challenge me because the lessons were those I'd learned in Primary. My knowledge of the gospel, I felt at the time, would not be furthered by my association with these gospel-disadvantaged souls.

My idea of success when I began teaching was to get to know the parents of my students. For that reason I loved back-to-school night at Box Elder High. That was a time when I could speak to doctors and lawyers and city officials about the welfare of their sons and daughters. Through this I had some status in the community.

But with the Navajo youngsters there would be none of that. Their parents were hundreds of miles away.

No, the work with these students was not for me. Next year, I reasoned, we'd get a new teacher. Then I'd have seniority over him. This new teacher would be assigned to take this unattractive assignment.

During the early part of the school year, some of my colleagues would say, "Don't you dream of teaching institute and advancing in the program?" They'd add, "Working with the Indians won't give you experience that will help you further your career. I don't see how you can teach those students. I want to see the fruits of my labors. I want to lift my students toward college. I want to work with students who will challenge me and cause me to grow."

Hearing such statements would bring me a bit of self-pity.

But little did I know.

As the weeks of autumn came and parted I made

some magnificent discoveries—discoveries that would change me forever.

It was true that in those days the larger portion of the students at the Intermountain Indian School were a bit timid when compared with "white men" standards. In addition to their quiet nature, many of them struggled with the English language. But I soon learned that they communicated in ways other than with many words.

As the first few weeks of teaching went by, I became aware that these young people had a special sense that allowed them to see in unusual ways. They seemed to strip aside all the layers of artificiality and to look into the souls of people and to the center of things.

Perhaps what I sensed that their brown eyes could see was more a product of my imagination than a reality. Maybe they couldn't see what I felt they could. But this I do know: These young folks had been compensated for what they lacked in verbal abilities by being given the ability to see the things that matter most.

After the first day of teaching at the Indian seminary I knew that my sense of humor, which helped me so much in my relationships with the Box Elder students, was not of much worth to the young Navajos. Nor were they much interested in my sports stories and my teenage experiences. All they seemed to respond to was that little leftover portion of me that was not part of my outgoing personality. All I had left was my humility, my gentleness, my kindness, and my love. And that was all they wanted.

So I tried—oh, how I tried—to shine forth in those qualities. I tried not to put on shows but to somehow show the deep things that I felt.

With them I had to specialize in simplicity. I

sought ideas that would not be the hit of a faculty seminar or symposium but that might, if coupled with the Spirit, make a hit in a young Lamanite's heart. I sought continually for pure truth and for ways to take that truth from my heart and help it into theirs. The only reward I knew while I taught there was a very private reward—it was the satisfaction of knowing that once in a while I was an A teacher. Not a publically recognized A teacher, but an undiscovered A teacher. A teacher who would be lost in a quiet, secluded classroom. A teacher who would just be observed by the only father who ever came to the Indian back-to-school night—the Father who is the father of us all.

I cannot tell all of the experiences I had while surrounded by my Lamanite friends, but I can tell some.

Once I saw Ed Brown, with whom I team-taught one class, do something I'll forever remember. He addressed a girl on the front row and bore testimony directly to her of the love Heavenly Father had for her. She didn't look up. She was so timid that she never looked up in class. Wanting so much to look into her eyes, Ed knelt down in front of her. Looking directly into her downcast eyes, he said, "Emily, Heavenly Father loves you, and so do I."

Sixteen-year-old Emily felt his words, and later, as I took my turn teaching, she looked up. I'd list that magic moment when Ed taught with eye-to-eye contact as the finest teaching moment I'd ever seen.

I recall fifteen-year-old Jimmy. He was a trouble-maker and wasn't shy by any standards. His boisterousness was downright disruptive not only to his own class but to our other seven classes. Jimmy would never listen to a lesson.

About midyear I decided that I as a teacher was

saying too much and the students were saying too little in our lessons. The only answers they ever gave were "yes" or "no." I decided that I would change that. I'd get them to talk. So on a special day I said, "I brought some popcorn today. Let's all sit around and eat it, and as we eat we'll talk about what Heavenly Father is like."

I set the stage as well as I could and then softly said, "Now, you each tell me what you feel about our Heavenly Father." For a few minutes all was silent except for the crunching of popcorn.

I gently said, "Robert, do you believe in Heavenly Father?"

The only response I got was some crunching.

"Albert, what about you?"

More seconds of silence, except for crunching.

I gently asked, "Albert, do you believe in a Heavenly Father?"

More silence followed. But then Albert said softly, "Yes."

I asked, "Why?"

After a pause he spoke again. "Because I was in a car and it went off the road, and just before we crashed I prayed nobody would get hurt, and nobody did."

Soon Roy added that he believed in God because his mother had been sick and he prayed and she got better.

The momentum caused nearly all to join in. Even Jimmy was caught up in the sweet comments being made.

Soon we talked of Jesus. Sadie said, "Jesus is bread and water."

I asked, "Why is that?"

She replied, "Because that is what we have in the sacrament."

I explained about the sacrament, and when I finished she said, "Oh," with understanding.

For several weeks we taught in this way of letting these young people make soul-to-soul comments. Then we had a testimony meeting with all the classes together. There the students took turns expressing their feelings.

At this meeting one would get up and slowly walk up to the front. Incidentally, those students could really walk slowly. All would watch as one made his or her journey to the pulpit. That person would say a few sentences of testimony, and all would watch until he or she had returned to sit down. We spent much of our meeting engaged in travel time.

Finally, toward the end of our time together, on the back row Jimmy stood. Those seeing him stand softly snickered. Jimmy was a clown, and they all laughed a good amount at just about everything he did.

Everyone watched as this strikingly handsome young man in his Levi jacket swaggered his way to the front.

As he held the pulpit with both hands, leaned back, and looked out, a complete silence filled the chapel. All seemed to wonder at once, What funny thing will Jimmy say? I, along with the others, held my breath in anticipation.

After a few seconds our wonder ended as Jimmy's voice rang out. He said, "Something strange is going on up here at LDS seminary. I've been coming up here for three years. In all that time, everything the teacher says goes in this ear [he pointed at his left ear] and comes out here [pointing to his right ear]." Jimmy paused for several seconds.

Finally he spoke again. "But lately a strange thing has been going on. What my teacher says goes in here [again he pointed at his ear], but," he said as he put his hand on his heart, "it has been stopping right here."

There was no laughing. Jimmy the clown was now Jimmy the teacher. As he expressed his feelings about heavenly things, the Spirit of the Lord testified to all of us that what Jimmy said was true.

If anyone ever said or thought there were no rewards in teaching the truly humble folks, the ones not in the limelight, then I wish they could have been in that chapel that day.

Public praise might come to some teachers; some may be "teachers of the year" or get praised by their honor students' valedictory remarks at graduation. But the praise that really matters is the unspoken kind that comes to a teacher when he or she knows that those things that go in ears or eyes have fallen solidly and everlastingly into some students' hearts. And that makes it so that the sky that is in the heart becomes more blue, and the foreground gently becomes closer to the beauty of the sky.

17

Seeing Some Evil in the Foreground but None in the Sky

Winning athletes know that if you think you are going to lose, you are usually right.

The most profound contest of all that is going on today is not any athletic event or even a war. Instead, it is the contest found everywhere—the contest between good and evil. If we who are key players in this contest decide that evil will win, that could be considered an evil thought, for it could help evil to win.

Our students are also key players in the contest between good and evil. If we think they are lining up on the evil side of the ball, then that thought could help them do so. But if we see them on the good side, that will help us help them actually be on that side.

In my better moments I find myself feeling supreme joy for the honor of being associated with the noble ones who are my students. Oh, I know they have problems. A first, second, third, fourth, and even a fifth glance reveals that many of them have sad, confused, timid, haughty, or even strange foregrounds. But oh, what skies they have! It is fun and inspiring to just imagine what might happen if they each became what they could be.

The most exciting classes of all are those made up of students who have fouled-up foregrounds.

I recall such a class at my ward. I was president of the Young Men. My biggest problem was that no one was willing to teach the teenage boys each Tuesday evening. I finally told the bishop that if he would release me, he could easily get a new president. Then I could go to where the wild things were and teach them.

I was glad when he agreed, because there was something about this group of guys that really fascinated me. They were unlike any group I'd ever known. At that time there was a tremendous drive among the young folks to be "cool," and this group really considered themselves to be cool. Somehow I got a kick out of that because I thought that as far as I understood the word *cool,* these guys really were. And the more they thought it, the more it seemed to be so.

I was anxious to teach them. I didn't have some notion I'd shape them all up and take away their cool. I think mostly I just wanted to see if I could understand what made them the way they were.

The first night I had a good lesson prepared. It wasn't a highfalutin lesson way above their world. It was down to earth, with just an occasional look toward heaven. But when I presented the lesson, I found that even that was too religious for my young friends. Our discussion soon devolved into almost exclusively worldly subjects.

So I decided to be the discussion moderator. I'd insist that only one speak at a time and that we all stay on the same subject until it was exhausted and then move on.

They were fascinating teachers—or, I should say, students. I recall that one night we talked about the police officer who worked in the halls of their school. I found that fascinating, because when I went to school we didn't have a police officer. We talked of the qualities a good police officer should have. At the end of our hour, just before we went to play basketball, I asked them if I could take a minute and say something. They agreed, and I said, "You know, I've loved being here with you tonight, and I'm so glad that you guys don't have any problems that would involve a bad relationship with any police officers. I'm proud of you. And I love you." They were all silent. I shouted, "Now, let's go play basketball!"

The next week when we were in our classroom, my cool young friends told me all about drugs. It was quite an education for me as they told me what they had observed in the way of drug users. Again they let me conclude the discussion. This time I said, "Thank you for teaching me about the effects and dangers of drugs. I am so glad that you men are wise and strong and that you steer clear of drugs. I love you guys, and you each can be a great leader. Now, let's go play ball."

I liked these guys. I mean, I really liked them.

In the next class, one of them got us going by telling us a communist kid had a locker next to his. They all told me what they thought of communism and capitalism. It was interesting to me because when I was in high school, there wasn't a single communist in my class. None of us in those days even knew what a communist was.

The next week there wasn't room for all of the guys who came in the classroom, because several young men were coming from another ward. I told them they ought to go to their own ward. One replied, "We don't like going there. The teacher there is always prepared, and you never are. That's why we like coming here." I wondered if that was a compliment.

As I write this, I can see those guys in my mind. Oh, how I loved them! To me they were great. We talked of many problems faced by young people, such as pornography, alcohol, speeding cars, and cops. At the end of each discussion, I'd ask for my moment.

One time, after a discussion on driving, I asked one, "Do you speed?"

"No, my old man would kill me if I did," he replied.

"I know your dad," I said. "He's my friend. He's a great man, and he is so blessed to have a son like you." As I described his father, my big "cool" friend struggled to hold back his tears.

Another who wore big black boots and rode a motorcycle asked, "Brother Durrant, what's wrong with drinking coffee?"

I looked at him as he sat back on his chair with its back tilted against the wall. He continued, "Each day I sluff my third-hour class and go to a cafe to drink coffee, and it don't hurt me."

I asked, "How old are you?"

"Sixteen."

"What priesthood office do you hold?"

"Deacon."

"You're sixteen years old and you're a deacon, and you want to know what's wrong with drinking coffee?"

I kicked his boot with my foot, and it knocked his foot off from where it rested on his other knee. This caused his chair to slam down onto all four of its legs.

Startled, he said, "You don't have to get mad."

I replied, "I am mad. I'm mad at what you're doing with your life. Get on the ball. Be what you can be."

I softened and said, "I love you. It hurts me when you don't do all you can do. I love all you guys. I'm glad we're friends—that's why I want you to shape up and look at the sky and be somebody." I paused and looked at each one. Then I clapped my hands and said, "Now, let's go play softball."

As we journeyed a block or so to the softball field, I walked close to the troubled one.

"I want to say the closing prayer at your missionary farewell," I said.

"What?" he said laughingly. "I ain't goin' on no mission."

"I didn't say anything about your going. I just want to give the closing prayer at your farewell when you go."

"How can you if I ain't goin'?"

In the weeks that followed, each time I'd see him he'd say, "Are you still going to give the closing prayer at my farewell?"

I'd say, "I sure am."

"How can you? I ain't goin'."

Three years later I was serving as mission president in Kentucky. That student called one night and said, "Can you come home?" I asked him why. He said, "'Cause it's my missionary farewell, and you said you'd give the closing prayer."

Many years have passed since those sacred times when I met with the "cool" ones. As I think back, I realize what a glorious time that was.

I didn't teach them much. But I think they knew I couldn't see any evil in them, only good.

I think they knew I could see beyond their foreground and into their sky.

We teachers need to see the sky in our students. When we do, everything can work together for the good.

18

Rejoicing in the Truth Reveals the Purest Sky

Remember when, earlier in this book, I spoke of the day I imagined the earth stood still while I taught my ninth graders about the law of chastity? How much did I really succeed? As I said, I was so keyed up that day, so determined to force my message into their hearts, that it didn't go as well as I had hoped it would. It was a good B effort, but I had longed for that to be an A day. I was disappointed when I tried so hard and, instead of hitting the nail on the head, I sort of bent the nail over. Nonetheless, I accomplished some things, and I laid a foundation for other things that I hoped would come later.

Several days after that lesson, an opportunity came. I didn't plan for it. I didn't set anything up. It just happened.

An ambulance passed by our classroom with its siren drowning out my voice. As its sound faded we all felt a bit sober, and each wondered who was so dramatically in need of medical help.

My mind and heart were changed as I wondered where the ambulance was headed and at whose house it would stop. My heart was full as I looked out at my thirty young students. Without thinking of what to say, I spoke:

"Oh, my dear friends, last Saturday while I was shoveling snow in my driveway I heard, way off in the distance, the sound we just heard pass by out the window. Then, as now, I wondered who was sick or hurt. As I wondered who so desperately needed help, I thought of you—each of you.

"I paused there in the snow and silently prayed, 'Oh, dear Heavenly Father, please make it so that the ambulance is not headed toward one of my students, because, Heavenly Father, each of them is so dear to me.'

"As I stood there in the cold air I looked up into the clear blue winter sky, and I longed for each of you to be safe—not just safe from an accident or illness, but safe from sin.

"To me you are all so pure. Keep yourselves pure. We talked last week of living virtuous and chaste lives. Keep yourselves pure. Be careful, my dear friends. You have so much ahead of you. Keep yourselves pure."

Silence filled the room as my eyes swept from one to another of my friends. I paused as I looked at each one for just a second or so—just long enough to seal what we both felt in the sacred moment when we understood what really mattered and we rejoiced together.

But now it was time to teach a less delicate commandment: "Thou shalt not steal."

Students in all ages of time have been tempted to cheat on a test or other schoolwork. I supposed a lesson on that would be useful, for cheating is indeed stealing—it is taking something that hasn't been earned.

My desire to be a bit creative led me to a rather dramatic approach. This became my lesson plan: I would announce to the class that grading time was fast approaching and that I didn't have enough information to determine what grade each of them should receive. For that reason I had decided to go against what I had formerly promised and would now give them a surprise test.

I soberly announced that this test would count for 90 percent of their grades. I told them that the questions would be very difficult, but that each of them would have an equal chance and so it would be fair.

I wrote three confusing essay questions on the board and told them to begin. I advised them that because of the importance of their scores, each student should be absolutely honest.

I had previously asked another teacher to come in at that point of time in the class period and call me to the telephone.

Earlier I had let two students in on my plan, and I had told them to walk around the classroom blatantly looking at other students' papers and to use their own books and notes to search for answers. After I left, the two began to do these dishonest activities.

When I returned after some fifteen minutes away, the class was very somber. I told them to read from their scriptures while I collected and read the test papers. The questions had been so strange that none but the cheaters had the correct answers.

I then stood and said, "I'm disappointed that only Jim and Steve [the ones I'd told to cheat] have answered the questions correctly."

The rest of the students sat in stunned silence. Some were in tears. I asked them why they were concerned and told them that they each had had an equal chance with the boys who had done so well.

As I stood silently at the front, a girl softly said, "Brother Durrant, Jim and Steve cheated."

I tried to act indignant. "So just because they did well, you say they cheated?"

Again there was a foreboding silence. A boy, without looking up, said, "They did cheat." Soon others joined in the now unanimous accusation.

I asked the two boys, now so condemned, to leave because they had tried to steal a score they had not earned.

After the boys were gone for a moment, I invited them back and announced that the whole experience was a big fake. I thought that the discussion which would follow would teach an unforgettable lesson—but it didn't. The only thing any of them seemed to be thinking of was the deep hurt they felt at the stealing I had done from them by violating their trust.

That day I was not an A, B, or C teacher. That day I was a deceitful teacher, for I had told a lie in an attempt to teach the truth, and that just doesn't work.

I don't think those students really ever saw me quite the same after that day.

I determined that never again would I fiddle around with the truth. And in defense of myself, I have always thereafter taught and rejoiced in pure truth. I don't even bend on April 1.

I am now a college teacher. Many college students like to write letters to newspapers and love to have heated discussions on current issues.

One day, as I walked from my classroom back to my office, I was joined by a student.

"Brother Durrant," he said, "many students are influenced by your words. Why don't you get into the issues and set some of these people straight?"

"Oh," I said, "I talk about the issues each day. I speak of abortion by speaking of the pre-earth life and of the beauty of being born on this beautiful earth and living God's plan. I speak of all the issues by speaking of the doctrine that tells us the way things should be. I speak of the critics and debunkers by speaking of the beauty and reality of love at home and the power of prayer and the joy of following the Lord and his leaders."

I further explained that time is so short in the classroom that I can't afford to speak of that which is not good, because I have scarcely enough time to tell even a hundredth part of the joy I feel in trying to tell of the happiness to which the truth can lead us.

I don't know if he understood. But sometimes endless debates viewed outside gospel light are like the debate over the greater importance of the sun or the moon. The person arguing for the moon won the debate by stating that the moon shines at night when it is needed—the sun only shines in the daytime when it is light anyway. Some issues need greater understanding than that which can be generated in a room with four walls and no opening through which to gaze toward heaven.

When we speak the truth as we feel it in our

hearts, and when we try with all our souls to live in accordance with truth, when we rejoice in truth and know that there is no spirit of truth in bitterness, sarcasm, or cynicism, then we will have those kinds of moments my class had when the ambulance passed by our classroom window. For a moment we will feel God's love in our hearts, and we will see the sky.

19

Helping Them Gain the Confidence to Reach into the Sky

DWIGHT Q. DURRANT

As I was growing up, I often heard my father speak to various groups. He seemed to possess great self-confidence. He would tell the audience just how handsome he was—I think he had to tell them because it wasn't readily apparent. He would state that going on a mission made a man more handsome, and then he would point out that he had been on three missions.

Despite the overwhelming evidence to the contrary, I still believed that this conviction of my dad's was true. Often in high school I would look in the mirror and say to myself, *I gotta go on a mission.*

Finally, the time came for me to go. I worked as hard as I could to ensure that my mission would be successful—and I also hoped that one of the lesser products of my labor would be that I would be more handsome.

When my mission ended, my father was among those who greeted me at the airport. It was so good to see my family again, but there remained a lingering question: had my mission done the trick?

"Well, Dad," I asked, "has my mission made me handsome?"

I still remember his looking at me from head to toe and then saying, "Well, son, I guess that theory doesn't work in all cases.

"But," he quickly added, "you don't need to be good-looking to look good. And, my son, you sure do look good."

Among the many qualities of a good teacher is the ability to help the students look good because they are good. I have had a special interest as a teacher in building the self-esteem of my students. I've done so because I know that in my own life and in the lives of others, the confidence level is the number one factor that determines success or failure. I feel that helping to improve the students' confidence is among the most important things a teacher can do. Thus, a teacher should be aware, as he moves through the important subject matter, that he can also be doing things that will positively influence each student's self-confidence.

Many of those we teach already possess a good deal of confidence in their ability to learn, socialize, or practice some skill. However, there is another type of self-confidence that is more difficult to detect: spiritual confidence. When I was in my teenage years I sometimes wondered, *If I were to die today, would I make it to the celestial kingdom?* The answer in my mind was always no. For some reason I felt I had to be nearly perfect to have a chance of making it, for "few there be that find it."

But now, as I reflect back to my teenage years and in retrospect try to answer that question, I have a feeling that if I had died as a teenager I would have had a very good chance of making it. So why did I feel there was no way?

I teach seminary now, and I think most of my students feel the same way I did. One day I asked them to respond anonymously on a piece of paper to the question: "How many of you feel that if you died today you would make it to the celestial kingdom?" Not a single person responded that they felt they would make it. They had the impression that eternal life was just too hard to obtain—there were too many things they had to do and be.

As I teach, I try to put things within reach of my students. If they perceive things to be too lofty or too hard to reach, they might never even try to reach out and grasp them. I don't lower the standards in my teaching so that living the gospel appears easier; rather, I try to do and say those things that will help the students feel more confident that they can reach the highest heights—their celestial skies.

Jesus Christ was a master at strengthening and building the spiritual and even temporal confidence of those around him. A story that illustrates this is found in chapter 14 of Matthew.

Jesus had just fed the multitude and had sent his disciples to sea while he went to a mountain to be with his Father. That night he walked on top of the water to join his disciples in the ship. When they saw him coming toward them, they were very fearful, thinking him to be a spirit. Immediately he calmed their fears with the words, "Be of good cheer; it is I; be not afraid."

In our own lives these same words from the Savior have profound implications. He is with us. He is on our side. To us he says, "Be not afraid."

Peter, seeing this great miracle of walking on water, wanted to do the same. The Savior didn't say, "No way, Peter. I'm the only one who can do this. You aren't capable." The Savior said, in essence, "Come on out of the ship. You can do it, Peter; I know you can. Don't be afraid." With the confidence Jesus had helped him build, Peter stepped out of the boat, and he was able to walk on water.

Can you imagine the faith it took to take that first step, followed by the thrilling reassurance that he was not sinking? But then, as Peter walked toward Jesus, he began to look around him. He felt the wind and saw the waves. Suddenly he began to doubt. His confidence left him, and he began to sink. In a panic he cried out to his Friend to save him. Immediately Jesus reached out, grasped his hand, and lifted him up to the surface of the water. Then, with Jesus at Peter's side, the two walked back to the ship.

My students, and yours, are much like Peter. They may not want to walk on water, but they do want to do things that are difficult for them. They want to do good. They want to succeed. But sometimes life gets tough, and the wind starts to blow and the waves get big all around them. It's natural that they then doubt and start to sink, but, as teachers we can put out our hands and give them the confidence they need to rise and stay on top. We can help them find the strength they need to be able to succeed in things which, in their young lives, are almost as difficult as walking on water.

Spiritual confidence comes as we repent and live more fully the principles of the gospel. A vital thing a teacher can do to help students build their self-confidence is to encourage them to live in accordance with the principles Jesus taught. Those who teach the gospel need to make Christ the central point of all their lessons. Those who teach in classes where they can't speak of religious concepts still need to encourage students to do better in all things. I've encouraged my students to live moral, productive, service-centered lives. As they do so, I see them begin to feel a sense of hope in their lives, and spiritual confidence begins to grow.

I recall my father teaching me the important principle of honesty. When I was sixteen I got a job bagging groceries at a local grocery store. I will openly admit that I hated this job. I wanted to be doing something else.

One morning a friend called and invited me to go waterskiing. I love waterskiing, but I was scheduled to work that day. My friend told me to do what a lot of people do when they don't want to go to work: call in sick. The idea appealed to me, especially if it meant a day on the lake.

I called my boss, altering my voice to make myself sound sick. It worked. I was now free to go. However, I worried about being caught in my lie, so I told my little sister Sarah to tell anyone who called that I was sick in bed and couldn't come to the phone.

It was a beautiful day on the lake, and I had a great time. When I arrived home I was greeted by my sister Sarah, who informed me, in a voice that told me I was in trouble, that Dad wanted to talk to me.

I went out back where Dad was working in the garden. He asked me where I had been, and then where I was supposed to have been. I knew he knew, so I confessed. He told me that when he came home from work, the phone rang. Sarah answered and told one of my friends that I was sick in bed and couldn't come to the phone. Dad said, "Not only did you lie to your boss, but even worse, you have made your little sister lie for you."

It was then that I began to feel bad. Dad made me feel worse by telling me that he thought I should apologize to my sister and write my boss a letter telling him of my dishonesty. That was the last thing I wanted to do, but I knew it was what I should do.

After the excruciating task of forming the letter, I took it outside to show it to my father. He then came up with another bad idea: he would drive me down to my boss's house so that I could personally deliver the letter. I suffered much as he drove me down in silence. Much to my relief, my boss wasn't home. I left the letter and continued to suffer, waiting to hear from him.

Early the next morning, the phone rang. My boss invited me to come in and talk to him. (I must admit that I was hoping some good would come of this and perhaps I would be fired.) My boss was very kind and understanding, and he assured me that I could be honest in the future if I ever wanted a day off.

I learned some great lessons in all this. I learned what it meant to be completely honest, and though I can't say I have always been so since then, I can say that I have never and will never call in sick again unless I really am. With my father's help I repented, and I knew that I would never do it again. I felt much better about myself when all of this was resolved. My spiritual confidence was greatly increased.

I've observed the way my students feel about themselves. They have a need to feel loved. It is not enough to *be* loved—they have to *feel* loved. They also need to feel that they are of some worth. I recognize that as a teacher I need to do all I can to help my students satisfy this need.

Doctrine and Covenants 18:10 states, "The worth of souls is great in the sight of God." At least, that's the way it is usually quoted. What is perhaps the most important word in the verse is usually left out. The actual verse reads, "Remember, the worth of souls is great in the sight of God." As a teacher, I try to keep in mind that each of my students has great worth. The problem is that sometimes I don't *remember* this. I fail to treat them and deal with them in keeping with the worth of their souls. If I don't constantly remember their great worth, I know that I might give one of them the message that he or she is of little worth.

The key to helping students feel they are loved and of great worth is to love them. I know that if I do not truly love the students, or, as Paul said, feel charity for them, it will be nearly impossible for me to help them feel loved. As I've taught I've found it is easy to love most of my students. However, there are some who are more difficult for me to love. It is ironic that these are the ones who often need my love the most. These are the ones who don't have a clear view of the sky. Often they have lost hope. As difficult as it may be, I try to reach out to them with love. As I do that, I feel—and they do also—that my words ring true.

I have listed some things that have helped me as I teach. Maybe they will help you too.

—I express love and appreciation often.
—I talk to my students before and after each class so that each one will feel that I know

him or her and treasure our relationship. As I do this, I briefly mention the interests of each student. This helps me to have meaningful conversations with them and to really get to know each one of them.

—I make personal contact with each student during the class by looking into the eyes of each as I teach. I call on them by name during the course of the class.

—I try to trust my students. This is difficult, because sometimes some of them are not worthy of trust. I feel that I can help each one be more trustworthy by increasing the amount of trust I place in them.

—I try to compliment each one as often as is reasonably possible. I make certain my compliments are sincere, which makes my words meaningful to each student.

—I force myself to praise more than I criticize. Students do far more good things than they do bad and should be praised far more than they are criticized.

—I write notes of praise and encouragement to my students.

—I allow students opportunities to express their opinions and feelings.

These are a few of the ways I try to help students gain confidence. By remembering the great worth of each student, I feel great joy and gratitude in being their teacher.

20

Oh My,
I Can See Your Sky!

As I conclude the writing of this book, my heart is full. I've exerted all the energy of my soul to try to adequately express my feelings relating to the sacred subject of teaching. I hope that what I have written has been clear and understandable. I hope that it has aided you in seeing the sky of those you teach and in seeing the personal possibility revealed in your own sky. Oh, how I hope that each one of you who is young and wonders about what you will do for a life's work will choose to be a teacher!

A teacher! Just saying that word causes a joyous sensation to surge through my soul. By the word *teacher* I don't mean an ordinary teacher. Rather, I use the word in a more sacred manner. When I say *teacher* I mean a noble person who has a wealth of knowledge about subject matter and who, in addition, immerses himself or herself in charity—a person who cares, more than can be expressed, about the destiny of those he or she is privileged to teach.

Please, young folks, consider the life of a teacher. Some of you know in your heart that you should teach. But you say, "I can earn so much more going down another road." Of course, that is a possibility if we are talking of dollars. But if we are speaking of satisfaction and fulfillment, then there is quite a living to be earned in teaching.

Last week I was teaching (just writing that sentence caused happiness to fill my heart to overflowing)—I repeat, last week I was teaching, and as I was explaining a principle I felt a thought deep down inside of me. I have learned that such thoughts can be a foundation for a sincere vocal expression, and so, a second later, I expressed what I had felt by saying: "My friends, you all understand that I get paid for being your teacher. It's a job for me, and it's the way I earn a living. But there is something else you should know—there's something extra I do that I don't get paid for, and that extra something is the feeling of love and deep respect I feel for you. Those feelings go far beyond any duty or responsibility for which I am paid. And it is those extra feelings I have for you that bring me such joy and that make me love being a teacher."

After pausing I concluded: "Some of you should be teachers, and then you could have a bunch of young friends that you could love and honor as I do you." I quickly returned to my original subject, for I feared my delicate feelings for my students and for teaching would flood my eyes and dampen my notes.

Not long ago I met a young student named

Dawn. As we became acquainted I asked her about her family. I learned that though her family lived in the East, they were originally from Utah. Dawn said her grandfather had once taught school in American Fork. I asked her his name and her answer almost took my breath away, for she said, "His name was Rulon Brimhall."

"Mr. Brimhall was your grandfather," I said reverently. I then added, "He was my teacher. He was my teacher." I related to her the story of my door-closing career and of the deer hindquarters—the very stories I recorded earlier in this book. Dawn was touched, and we shared many more words about our common love for her grandfather and my teacher, Mr. Brimhall.

She could have said, "My grandfather was the governor of Utah," and I would have been impressed. She could have said, "My grandfather was an all-American football player at BYU," and I would have really been impressed. But when she said her grandfather was Rulon Brimhall, I was far beyond the limits of where the word *impressed* can reach.

Recently I saw a fellow who grew up in American Fork—my hometown. I told him, "I'm writing a book about teaching, and in it I speak of your father. I wish he were still living so I could let him see what I've written." His eyes moistened and so did mine as a feeling of love went between us. You see, his father was my teacher: Mr. Sorensen. He's the one whom I mentioned earlier, the one who made me feel I was his favorite—the one who treated me as a friend. He found me when I was halfway to nowhere and showed me my sky and helped me find a path to my somewhere.

I have sons and daughters who, largely because of their mother, are nice-looking and have achieved good things in life. One is a lawyer. One is a businessman. One is a manager. And one is a student and athlete. Three are magnificent full-time homemakers. I, of course, love them all equally.

But I have one son who is a teacher. He helped me write this book. His name is Dwight, but his students call him Brother Durrant. He and his wife, Marci, and their two little girls currently live in Vernal, Utah. Their house is small because they can't afford a bigger one, but Dwight's blessings stretch forth from border to border of the beautiful Ashley Valley.

My other sons and daughters weren't cut out to be teachers; their inclinations led them down other roads. But Dwight knew that his heart was inclined to teaching. He is like the fellow I wrote about earlier in this book—the man who beat me in a one-on-one basketball game on a night many years ago. Dwight could beat his students just as that man beat me. Dwight's students love him just as I loved that teacher. But you remember that that man turned and walked away from me and those like me.

Dwight didn't walk away. He walks right into the middle of the young ones and loves them and teaches them. Dwight followed his heart and went to where the students were. He and I love to talk about the sometimes confused foregrounds and the beautiful skies of the young ones.

Lest I be too hard on that teacher who walked away, I say that I'm sure he has still spent much time as a teacher. It is impossible to live life without being placed in a position where we are teachers. In the work world we are teachers to those we supervise, train, or manage, or to those who supervise, train, or manage us. All appropriate relationships pass the baton of teaching back and forth, almost like a game of tag. We teach, and then the other person becomes "it" and he or she teaches us.

As parents we teach, and if we desire we can point out the sky to our children far more clearly than can any other teacher.

Come to think of it, Mr. Paul's advice to teachers really fits parents. I know that as a parent I could provide every material blessing for my children, but if I didn't provide love I'd be nothing—or at least, I wouldn't be what I ought to be.

If I preached to my children with the tongue of an angel and did not act in harmony with what I taught, then I would be to them as sounding brass or a tinkling cymbal. I know that as a parent I must at times suffer long as I relate to their undesirable foregrounds. Of course, I realize that sometimes because I struggle as a parent my children might have to suffer long also. But by sticking with it and not giving up when things are tough, we as a family, through our struggles and our joys, will see our individual and family skies, and then we will know that we have taught each other and that all has been worthwhile.

In no place can we become so easily provoked as we can at home. We can put up with much more from other people's children than we can from our own, but there is no place where being regularly provoked is as damaging as it is at home. It almost seems that if we as parents can avoid being provoked, we stand on the ground whereon a whole multitude of problems can be solved.

If we can honor our children as we hope they will honor us, we can make it together. But if we vaunt ourselves and act as though only our opinion matters, then rebellion lurks on our doorstep and soon enters our home.

Seeing the good in our children can blind us to any bad in them, and that is not always good, for we need to see their faults just as we do our own. But if their foreground faults loom so large in our eyes that we can't see their skies, then we are going contrary to Paul's words, "thinketh no evil."

Lastly, if we as parents strive to teach the truth by word and, more important, by rejoicing in truth, then our children will not obey because they have to but because they want to—they want to be happy as they see us rejoicing in our way of life. So either professionally, in other life's work, or as parents, we are all teachers.

We are privileged to teach others fact and theory about our universe. We can do this in an ordinary or in an extraordinary way. We can simply be teachers, or we can be master teachers. So why not point up instead of down? Why not say, "Oh my, I can see your sky, and it is beautiful!"